THE DIARY OF AN OBEDIENT WIFE

Karola Woods

Printed by CreateSpace and available on Amazon and other online stores.

First edition published in the United Kingdom 2017 by Karola Woods. Cover art by Karola Woods.

ISBN-13: 978-1979132121

ISBN-10: 1979132127

www.twitter.com/karolawoods
www.facebook.com/writingkarola

Acknowledgements

The author would like to thank Suzanne Williams, Jayne Leaves, Paula Scott, Krys Gajda, Debs Georgiou, Lee Hills, Lynne Brown and Sue Savage for their help in the creation of this novel.

For my husband

Saturday 14 August

Noon

Some moth strips arrived this morning from Amazon. I ordered them last week when I saw a moth flutter out of Tim's wardrobe and then another one out of mine. With Tim at work, and me still having painter's block (could really do with some inspiration there Lord, before my acrylics/oils/brain dries up), thought should do something useful and hang them up. As I opened my wardrobe, I found this list, printed out and stuck onto the inside, with Blu Tack that has long since lost its elasticity.

DO's
<u>What I will do when am married to Tim:</u>
Submit to him as unto the Lord
Put him first in all things
Always look beautiful (apart from first thing when hair is flat and have pillow-creased face) yet be more beautiful in character
Cultivate a quiet and gentle character of great worth in God's sight
Consider Tim better than myself
Tirelessly be his steadfast helper
Make lots of dinners for all kinds of people (even in-laws) and develop gift of hospitality
Find out his favourite dish then fine tune to perfection (make often, but not too often)
Pray for the gift of housework to be developed in me (use bee's wax where poss and hard green soap—also invest in a washboard)
Give to the poor (more than 20p)

Visit the sick (wearing mask if necessary)

Not let the sun go down on my anger, but live out 1 Corinthians 13, replacing the word 'love' with 'Emily'

Obtain authorisation for all purchases above £5 off Tim first (not because I have to, but because I humbly want an ordered household, just like the woman at the end of Proverbs)

Buy a spinning wheel and loom so like woman at end of Proverbs, can spin and weave our own purple linen (and maybe even socks)

Study Mrs Beeton's book on 19th century house management

Make everything out of Delia Smith's Complete Cookery Course and everything out of Julia Child's Mastering the Art of French Cooking (learn how to make bouillon from scratch and also, find out what it is. Think it involves boiling a carrot and a turnip for a very long time and then pressing it through a sieve)

Learn Heimlich manoeuvre for times when make steak and it turns out too tough

Iron not just shirts and tops but socks and underpants too

And finally, teach our rescued African Grey, Reginald, lots of Bible verses so that he can help us reach our lost friends, family and neighbours, of which there are many (and de-train him from all the expletives he knows from his previous owner).

DON'TS
<u>What I will not do when married to Tim:</u>

Nag or moan—lest any root of bitterness spring up and cause trouble
Be controlling or manipulative
Be rude, impatient or selfish (hardly ever am anyway, have patience of a saint)
I will not behave in such a way that makes Tim get a ladder and shin up it to sit on the corner of the roof
Wear scruffy clothes around the house, saying 'it's just us'
Yawn with my mouth open
Leave bits of old chewing gum around the house
Not let leg hair grow beyond 0.1 mm
Not find any film star attractive (change TV channel or walk out of cinema if do, confessing to Tim simultaneously)
Let ironing pile up.

The list hit me between the eyes like David's stone hit Goliath. I remember putting this up five years ago when we first got married. I was 34, Tim 37. I used to look at it a lot, then just a bit, then eventually, I forgot it was there.

I've done everything I said I wouldn't do Lord, and not done what I said I would! I have *not* submitted to Tim, I have answered back cleverly and often, even when he's right. I basically have the patience of a gnat.

I have *not* put him first in all things (particularly in the area of food, actually). All portions of chips must be divided exactly and if the number of chips isn't even, the odd one must be halved (I don't do this with rice though obviously, that would be excessive). Halving things goes for confectionary too. Once I weighed two halves of a Snickers on the electric scales to see if they were equal, then I shaved a bit of Tim's to add to mine.

I have given *some* money and possessions to the poor but only when I haven't wanted those things anyway, or when I've just been feeling too guilty to walk past yet another homeless person without doing anything.

I have bought *many* things without asking Tim first. I desperately wrestled with buying or not buying a steam mop from Aldi for ages but got one in the end, justifying it by saying it was an essential domestic purchase (used same excuse for a new lippy recently).

I have *not* visited the sick. In fact, I have actively avoided them. I hate getting people's colds. In fact I think there should be a law about people not leaving their houses if they have anything contagious.

I *have* let the sun go down my anger. I have gone to bed boiling mad but told myself I just 'need to let things settle'.

Have failed miserably on the old chewing-gum front too. In a recent attempt to clean the bathroom, found an old and hard chewed up blob balanced on a candle, hidden behind the wick and coated in dust (licked it clean, then decided there was life in it yet and popped it in my mouth).

Sometimes the hair on my legs is plaitable length.

Re finding celebrities attractive, I have caught myself feeling bitter that George Clooney isn't single anymore. Have even found myself trawling through the internet, trying to find a picture where his wife looks ugly (haven't found one as yet).

Re caring for people, I don't. At church, I actively avoid certain (many) members of the congregation (particularly the difficult ones, of which there are many). Have cultivated a look that goes out to infinity and looks very taken up with spiritual things (good way of avoiding eye contact with anyone).

Re cooking, yes I can do complex, but Mrs Beeton's household management book is currently a trivet and Julia Child's cookbook has long gone to the charity shop (much too difficult). Still no idea what *bouillon* is—I just enjoy saying it, over and over again.

Re Reginald—have managed to teach him some Bible verses but he still trots out the expletives—particularly when people from church come round (clear spiritual battle in heavenlies).

And when I come home after a shop, I often greet and hug Pluto and throw him his toy before greeting Tim!

Most disturbingly though Lord, I've realised that Tim has just bought a new set of ladders and of late, he has been up on the roof *rather a lot*.

I didn't take list down. I stared for it for ages.

It's our fifth anniversary this weekend, too, Lord.

Five years. In some ways, it feels like yesterday. In other ways, a lifetime.

Was going to put the list in the bin but then I thought….

No, Lord. I'll give it a try. So I proclaimed out loud:

Dear Lord, I hereby declare that from this moment on, I will once again try to be the perfect, obedient wife that I said I would be five years ago. May this diary reflect the mighty work You will do in me, Lord. Root out everything in me You want rooted out (although not sure what will be left once all rooting out is done). Amen.

Then I finished putting up all the moth strips and went to shave my legs.

Good things: Hanging up moth strips, rediscovering the list and doing my legs (on next shop, must see if Wilkinson's do a Ladies Machete).

Bad thing: Not keeping to list for best of five years.

QUESTION BEFORE THE LORD: While I'm at it, just what is it about moths and wool and silk, Lord? Of all the things for them to eat. They're so weird, like tiny old ladies flying around in heavy coats. And the way they come out at night to seek out light—why on earth did You make them that way? If they like the light so much, why don't they come out when it's day? Also Lord, are You OK with me killing a load of moths? It's not their fault they're moths, is it? I think they get a bad press compared to butterflies, yet they're not that different. I would go so far to say that butterflies are basically well-marketed moths. Although I suppose butterflies don't eat clothes, they fly around looking pretty, pollinating flowers. The alternative of doing nothing about the moths is having a major infestation where all our clothes are munched to bits and there are piles of moths lying on their backs patting their stomachs saying, 'That woolly cardi of his really hit the spot'. The Egyptians tried to stop their plagues in the Old Testament, didn't they? They didn't just welcome the locusts with open arms. Think have the common sense answer to my prayer Lord—will proceed with moth massacre. Just hope don't have pile of moth corpses to deal with over the next few weeks. Maybe I should also pack all these jumpers away as actually, just looking at them makes me feel hot.

Monday 16 August

Boiling outside. Been two days since I put the strips up but no moth corpses anywhere. My attempts to be the perfect wife, have, so far, not gone too badly. Got up early, made Tim a cooked yet non-greasy, balanced yet tasty breakfast which he guzzled with gusto, then saw him off with a packed lunch, dewy smile on face and a vintage and prayerful wave (must manicure nails as they look terrible). He looked distinctly puzzled as he cycled off down the lane.

His packed lunch consisted of chicken and chorizo sandwiches with a handful of rocket. He loves chorizo (rationed to few slithers though as very fatty). For the past few weeks, Tim's been walking around the house saying, 'I'm so thin! I'm so thin!' He has lost 12lb since he started cycling a year ago (I joined the gym at the same time but haven't lost a thing—in fact I think I have put weight *on*. Still, they say muscles weigh more than fat, don't they? So that must be it). Also called him Thinny a few times, which he liked, then asked him if I looked fat (he said no about a hundred times, but I still don't believe him).

Spent some time praising the Lord, as praise brings us into His courts—then tried to teach Reg to say, 'Praise the Lord.' He didn't say anything though, he just pecked at his mirror and shook his bell, which by faith, I will call praise.

Bound all spirits of painter's block and loosed all avalanches of creativity. Then went to canvas and stood there with my paint brush. Nothing. I need inspiration Lord. I could do something based on the Day of Judgement, or Easter, or even Christmas… the question is—what? I've had no commissions for ages, either. Perhaps I'd be better off going to paint the lounge? Sometimes I'm not sure if I like being an artist. I might have given up were it not for Tim, urging me on. Lots of people think it's just about flouncing around. But I know it isn't. It's about sweat, tears and lots of chocolate.

Good thing: Didn't tell Tim off for not putting his plate and bowl into the dishwasher. Remembered point on list about being his helper so put it in myself in meek submissive silence (although did rattle the drawer to show him that I'd done it so maybe it doesn't count).

Other good thing: Reginald came out with 'Praise the Lord' to Pat who popped round with a parcel she'd taken in while I was out.

Bad thing: As Pat was going, he promptly came out with a string of expletives too. Explained Reg is a rescue parrot and that he'd learned these profanities from his previous owner, not us (as we're CHRISTIANS). When she'd gone, prayed deliverance prayer over Reg, looking him in the eye.

Other bad thing: Have put on two pounds.

Tuesday 17 August

11am

Day 4 of being an obedient wife. Made Tim another cooked breakfast. It took ages actually, so not sure how long will be able to sustain this. Pluto was most interested when the sausages went under the grill, but he didn't get anything.

Managed to do my nails (one hand anyway). Then had a fry-up myself. Still not painting and still praying for inspiration. Did a couple of doodles on some envelopes though, a bit like Tracy Emin. But unlike Tracy Emin, I won't be able to sell mine for tens of thousands of pounds. I'll probably just throw them in the bin. My paintings online aren't selling either and when I did the accounts, I saw we are spending much more than we're earning.

Am starting to do a still life of bowl of fruit, as fruit always sells (surely). Have got an orange, some bananas and a pear. The bananas are starting to speckle dramatically in an End Times sort of way.

After breakfast, Tim asked why I was doing so much cooking and cleaning—was it because I wasn't able to paint? I looked down meekly (eye-lashes aflutter) and said, 'No lovely darling and dearest sweetheart, it's because I want to'.

Also Lord, am not wearing any jewellery because it's an external adornment and not a sign of inner unfading beauty (have gone off all my jewellery anyway and am desperate for some more).

OBEDIENCE RATING (O.R.) Because of cooked breakfasts, 9/10 surely.

The only snag is, am bit put out (livid actually) that Tim hasn't mentioned our anniversary this weekend. He said nothing yesterday and nothing today. It's just not like him Lord—he never forgets anything. Actually, that's not true. He forgets all kinds of things and it's really annoying. His phone (biggest offender), followed by his keys, money, packed lunches I've slogged over—and his phone charger.

'Have you seen my charger?' he says, every single day.

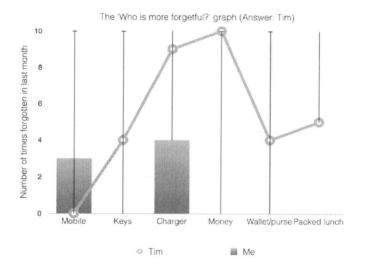

The 'Who is more forgetful?' graph (Answer: Tim)

I look around for a white wire, see several tangled on the table and say, 'Try over there'. Then I leave the room as soon as I can.

PRAYER BEFORE THE LORD: Lord, I hope that one day, houses are made with chargers in the walls, so they can never be removed.

I on the other hand, rarely lose anything. I label things, I file things, I have order in my life. I have designated places for things like phone-chargers. Actually, I have to admit I lost Tim on a visit to the British Museum once. Although I didn't really lose him, I just forgot he was with me as I was totally engrossed in the Egyptian mummies. They reminded me of Lazarus and how amazing it must have been for him to wake up from the dead in a tomb with Jesus outside calling out his name. Called, 'Tim, Tim, Tim,' for ages and even whistled a few times like I do for Pluto when I've lost him in the woods. In the end, I had to go the lost property to ask if anyone had handed him in. (They hadn't). Eventually, I found him near the loos, wandering around.

Just what am I meant to do re our anniversary Lord, given I want to be a perfect, submissive and godly wife?

Can't bark, 'What are we doing this weekend Tim, you've forgotten our anniversary, haven't you? And *when* are you going to get me some nice new jewellery/clothes because I'm starting to look like some kind of vagabond!'

I wanted to do a romantic painting for Tim of some kind, but at the moment, all I can do when standing at my canvas is either huff and puff, or cry.

Am I meant to remind him gently Lord, or trust that he'll remember? Perhaps he's planning a weekend away and he hasn't told me that he's whisking me away. I've just had a look at his calendar and he isn't on any rota at church. Perhaps he's booked us into a nice restaurant so that I don't have to cook? That'll be it. Wonder if I should cut down on my online Morrisons shop to pre-empt this, so that I don't overbuy? Or should I buy things I can freeze instead?

Or Lord, should I assume he *has* forgotten, not mention anything, but graciously cook a superb meal for two and casually say, 'Here's to five wonderful years darling,' as if have just remembered myself and an amazing meal is the norm? Surely that's the right thing to do? (Obedience Rating ascending rapidly).

PROPOSED PLAN OF ACTION BEFORE THE LORD: Will go to library and get some posh cookery books out. Have hoards already but can't find anything in them that inspires me. If Tim finds them and asks why have mountain of posh cook books, will not say a thing (though may do significant pause to give him a clue). Yes could look online, but there's something really homely about leafing through loads of outsize books while lying on the sofa with some chocolate and tea, Reg on my shoulder and Pluto by my feet. And every time I feel annoyed, I will proclaim: 'I do not feel annoyed or let down. Our love goes beyond man-made constructs and dates on a calendar. With the Lord, a day is like a thousand years and a thousand years a day'. In fact Lord, maybe that's it? Maybe Tim's perception of time is becoming more like Yours and to him, five earthly years seem like five seconds?

Good thing: Talking of chargers, have tackled the annoying nest of wires on our kitchen table while avoiding trying to paint (still producing nothing Lord and am running out of excuses when Tim asks what have been doing all day). Each phone charger is now stored inside its own bespoke odd sock, so that there are no wires anywhere. At first it was a bit ad hoc, i.e. any charger in either one of our socks, but then I refined the system, putting Tim's chargers in his odd socks, and my chargers in mine. The only problem is… I don't have odd socks as I store mine away properly so I've had to sacrifice a pair of mine to the project especially—but hey ho—no pain, no gain. (Don't know why haven't thought of this sooner, so it must be of You, Lord).

AREA OF GROWTH: Am clearly learning to lean on God more to sort out everyday problems. (O.R): 100/10, at least.

Have manicured other hand.

5.45pm

When Tim came back from work, he caught me sweeping up the kitchen floor with a dustpan and brush (not so much obedience, just a sure sign am stressed re forgotten anniversary).

Asked me how my painting was going—I said, 'Not too badly' (terribly, really). Felt like blatant lie so added was limbering up with a still life of some fruit (entirely true) and that it's entirely usual to work in this way—a bit like an Olympic runner cracking their knuckles and flexing their ankles before a record-breaking sprint. Then I pointed to the new charger sock storage system and explained how it's going to change our lives.

Dutifully listened to all his news about whose network had crashed when, but all could think was that he's forgotten our 'a'. Felt like screaming, 'You've forgotten our anniversary, haven't you Tim?' with the veins standing out on my neck like the Incredible Hulk. Also wanted to quote Ephesians 5 really loudly about husband's loving their wives as much as their own bodies (never really understood that scripture, Lord). But I didn't.

Have ransacked drawers for hidden gifts/cards/florist receipts but found nothing. Have also looked at his emails to see if there's anything confirming a restaurant or hotel. Nothing. Have also checked his web history—no jewellery or travel sites anywhere—just searches on cycling, cycling exercises, cycling clothes, cycling holidays and cycling gadgets. Oh, and a site for Miniature Schnauzers as Tim loves to find silly videos about Schnauzers that look just like Pluto—then he tells me to go and watch them too.

Home group at Stuart and Liz's tonight. In the flesh, am not in the mood—and my foot hurts too. I'm sure I've strained it in the gym, Lord. I never had any aches and pains until I joined that place. I thought they were meant to make you fitter?

QUESTION BEFORE THE LORD: Wonder who is on the cake rota at home group? If Eunice, will be homemade. If Pauline, shop bought.

MUST REMEMBER: Previous episodes of painter's block have been followed by periods of intense productivity. So maybe this blocking is a sign of eventual major and long-term outpouring?

Good thing: While exploring freezer contents to find out what we have in before doing major online shop for this weekend's 'by faith' 'a' meal, started a table of freezer contents so as not to end up with fish-fingers that are three years old or random bread crusts from former ancient loaves. Have also given each drawer a category e.g. breads/meat/vegetables/ready-meals/dessert-like items. Table is clipped onto board opposite fridge for handy ref. (My painter's block must be really bad).

Made Tim pancakes for dinner, his favourite. Since I've known him, Tim has gone on about loving pancakes more than anything else in the world so have finally made him some, albeit through gritted teeth. The first one was dud (universal law apparently, not sure why) but the rest were thin and crepey and looked like chammy-cloths (was tempted to try to use one on the windows actually, but thought best not). We filled them with grated cheese, ham and Worcestershire sauce, followed by lemon and sugar and then Nutella.

In spite of all 'a' bitterness, O. R. a definite 8/10.

AREA OF GROWTH: When I made the pancakes, I didn't have all the lights on like I normally do (Tim says it's like a football stadium in our kitchen and always switches half of them off). 'It's not like you Em, to cook in the dark,' he said as he came in. 'People change Tim,' I said, splattering Worcester sauce onto a pancake like I meant business.

OTHER QUESTION BEFORE THE LORD: Where exactly is Worcestershire anyway? It's one of those places I know nothing about like Warwickshire, Staffordshire, Hampshire, Herefordshire, Shropshire and while I'm at it, Wiltshire. Where are these places Lord, and what happens in them?

Bad thing: Obsessing about our 'a'. I hereby declare and proclaim that am going to stop now. I am really annoyed though.

10.30pm

Dear Lord. I repent of judging others for what they bring/bake for home group. As I thought, Pauline brought two packets of synthetic-looking muffins from some corner shop that looked as if they'd been sweating in their wrappers for about six months. Thought—thanks a lot Pauline, after all the cakes I've made from scratch for you/group, *this* is what you bring us, with your big servant heart?

During prayer, we got into pairs. Who was I paired with? Pauline! She prayed for my painter's block to go and for my poorly foot with such fervour that I felt thoroughly ashamed. Yes, she laid hands on the wrong foot (didn't have heart to say but main thing was she had contact with my body so bad foot would have been touched ultimately, though from afar). My foot is the same (sure things have changed in the spiritual realm though, and will soon manifest in the physical), but all cake judgement has *gone*, Lord.

Apart from that, home group was good. Stuart and Liz are great. If I want to be like someone when I'm older, it's them. They are kind and loving and Liz has an amazing ability to say no to pudding.

Bad thing: Liz has given us some frozen veggie burgers she bought by accident and doesn't want. Had mini-row with Tim on way home about where to put them in freezer (because of my new categorisation system.) Tim said to put them in the meat drawer as they resemble meat but I said they should go in the vegetable drawer as there isn't a shred of meat in them.

AREA OF GROWTH: In the end, I let go and let Tim put the burgers in the meat drawer. Conceded that they are fungi doing a very good impersonation of meat, and that they could therefore have the honorary position among the lamb, chicken, mince and sausages. NOTE TO SELF: Just when I thought I was doing really well at being obedient Lord, I trip up over Quorn! Have amended freezer chart accordingly.

WORST THING OF ALL: Tim says he's going out with the cycling lads this Saturday—i.e. on our anniversary weekend! Am devastated. What am I meant to do Lord? It's hard to be an obedient 'w' when you're annoyed with your 'h'. Five years is wood, apparently. I would have loved a new chopping board, had he remembered. One of those nice olive wood ones that are an unusual and smoothed-off shape and cost a whopping £50. If I had one right now, I expect I'd clonk him over the head with it.

THOUGHT BEFORE THE LORD: Wonder what my life would be like if I'd married Cliff Richard and not Tim? I know it's a long shot Lord, but it could have happened—and after five years, Cliff would probably be getting me something pretty fancy made out of wood e.g. a posh shed that I could use as an outdoor studio, with solar panels and lots of natural light. I could have met him in a church, or in London, or anywhere really. He could have just dropped a pile of lyrics in the rain. I'd have helped him pick them up—and the rest would have been history. Life would be so different if I were Mrs Richard. I'd spend half my time opening fan mail and looking after his diary probably, with the help of his record label. I'd have to make sure all his clothes were clean and nicely pressed—I mean really nicely pressed—not just any old how like I do for Tim—and I'd have to make sure I cooked low calorie things as he's lean and he needs to look his best all the time (I would need to look good all the time too, so impossible really). I'd have to get used to him singing around the house though which could either become annoying—or be fun, a bit like having my own personal jukebox I guess. I wouldn't need to put on You Tube to listen to Our Father or Living Doll, I could just ask him to sing them for me, with impressive variations. It would be hard going out with him anywhere public. Everywhere would have to be really exclusive and private (sure would

KAROLA WOODS

manage). I'd have to make sure that I had a posh pen on me at all times, so he could sign autographs and I'd have to defend him from besotted fans too, saying, 'Look, I'm his wife, he's taken, face it!!'

Wednesday 18 August

8.30am

What are the chances of this happening Lord? Put (OK, slammed) an already-opened carton of soup on the work top, ready for lunch later. A significant percentage shot up and out of the carton, going in the air, onto my head and on my white top. Where is the justice in that, Lord?

I wouldn't mind but there are some women in this world to whom this sort of thing never happens. Some women go out in their white tops, visit different people, have various meals (even things like spaghetti bolognese or sweet and sour chicken), go shopping, have coffee and still come home *clean*.

Seriously, I can watch a TV action drama where the female protagonist gets locked in a storage container for days with no sink or toilet, fights with a bad guy in mud, runs down a sewage tunnel to escape and drives a truck off a bridge into a ravine without so much as getting a single mark on her crisp white blouse. Me, I only have to go *near* jam or butter oil and I'm filthy (think need bib Lord).

I had a dream about our 'a' last night. I was cooking the most amazing roast dinner ever, a beautiful organic shoulder of lamb lovingly studded with cloves of garlic and spears of fresh rosemary, resting on a bed of finely chopped onions and juicy halved lemons. I sloshed Cinzano Bianco all over it with gay abandon and it made a heavenly smell permeate throughout the kitchen (amazing how realistic smells can be in dreams). Then I started expertly spooning parboiled Maris Piper potatoes into a tray of sizzling goose fat. Not a single, flesh-

16

burning, scream-eliciting spatter anywhere! Normally I maim myself with hot fat, risking permanent scarring.*

*Must start holding a sieve in front of my face to create a sort of shield—although it might look as if I'm about to go fencing.**

**Have always fancied taking up fencing, Lord. Maybe I should? I just love that white gear fencers wear and I think it would be such a thrill to run at someone hysterically with a sword and have them run at you (I'd jump out of the way though). Knowing my luck, I'd probably spill something down my white fencing outfit as soon as I put it on and look a total scruff. Plus I wouldn't look all tall and slender and mean, I'd look like Michelin woman.

In my 'a' dream, I popped the spuds into the oven and thought about how my roast potatoes made Delia's look like hard, underdone goose eggs—and knocked up some gravy which for once didn't have lumps in it that looked like tadpoles with their tales chopped off.

Seeing everything was completely under control, I walked into the hallway in a pair of red, 5-inch stiletto high-heels that I just happened to be wearing and had a look in the mirror. I looked stunning. Not a hair out of place, no gravy or toothpaste down my front or spinach on my teeth. Just enough time to sew a button on one of Tim's shirts like the woman at the end of Proverbs... when Tim appeared out of nowhere. He started kissing me passionately. At least I thought it was passionately. I then got woken up by Pluto licking my face.

SORRY LORD, I CAN'T HELP IT! IF TIM HAS FORGOTTEN OUR 'A', I'LL THROTTLE HIM, OBEDIENT WIFE OR NOT!

How can he go for a bike-ride on our big day Lord, *how*? His cycling gear is always everywhere Lord—as if a bicycle hurricane (a bicyclone?) has torn through our house, leaving a trail of cycling debris in its wake! Allen keys, inner tubes, lights, gloves, glasses, water bottles, weird outer shoes that make him look as if he's got hooves—and his long bib Lycra shorts that make him look like Popeye! I don't care about being obedient Lord, I just want him to remember our 'a' and not leave bike stuff around the house anymore. I'm forever tidying up after him Lord, forever! Agggggggggghhhhhhhhhhh!!!

11am

Have calmed down. Beat pillow and wept for a while and then took to reading James. Anger does not bring about the righteous life that You desire and I am now resigned to the fact Tim has forgotten the day we made our vows to one another and am accepting that You will work out Your higher purposes through the situation, pruning me of everything You want me to be pruned of, probably leaving a tiny stump.

Maybe You have let Tim forget because You want to drive false senses of security out of me, or You don't want me to bow down to a calendar date like some kind of Asherah pole, in the highest of high places?

Actually I've never really been that bothered about our anniversary before—it's Tim *forgetting* that has annoyed me. Perhaps it's a sign that we should go and visit someone in need? Or pick up some litter? There's certainly enough of it around. Or maybe we should pray together, with no mention of 'a's at any point whatsoever?

Mum's remembered our 'a' and sent us both sent us a card. Imogen's sent one too—but probably only because mum reminded her. I've hidden them in a drawer as I know that if Tim sees them, they'll jog his memory and I don't want to do that.

The good news is, I've suddenly started painting The Horseman of the Apocalypse. It started off this morning as a sort of enraged abstract, but then I thought I saw a horse emerge with a horseman on top, so I'm going with it. Perhaps the Lord is blessing me in my despair?

Just checked the drawers and wardrobes. No moth corpses anywhere, so am not sure what happens to them when they crash to the bottom of a pocket and die.

QUESTION BEFORE THE LORD: What happens to things like squirrels and birds and hedgehogs when they die Lord? I never see the lanes strewn with elderly squirrel or sparrow corpses. Perhaps they hide themselves away when they know it's their time? Or maybe they don't reach old age because we kill them off before in some other kind of way?

Bad thing: Apocalyptic horse looks like a panto horse now. Maybe a donkey is trying to come through Lord and it will morph into a Christmas scene or Balaam when his donkey rebukes him? Guide me, Lord, as I feel like giving up.

Other bad thing: Constantly looking at my phone. If I spent as much time in prayer as looking at my phone, I might actually change the world.

Good thing: After a reasonable morning painting, felt led to empty the larder of all out of date items and make a larder chart, just like for the freezer. Got rid of five carrier bags of stuff including three packets of royal icing from four years ago. I don't know what I bought them for Lord. Also threw out a bottle of mineral water. Label said, 'From sources that are thousands of years old. Expiry date—June'.

Yet another bad thing: Found peas in meat drawer and fish fingers in ice-cream and bread drawer (Probably Tim foraging for ice cream). Does he not realise the fridge freezer is a carefully balanced ecosystem?

Am making 5-spice Chinese duck breasts tonight. Am thoroughly enjoying reading lots of different web articles on searing the breasts in a pan then draining off the fat and finishing them off in the oven. Am also making Heston

Blumenthal golden syrup cookies. If one more chef tells me to grease my spoon before ladling out golden syrup as if they're telling me something I never knew already, I'll scream.

O.R: 10/10 for the huge amount of self-control am displaying with forgotten 'a'.

Good things: Duck breasts, cookies and pending End Times masterpiece. What more could Tim want?

DILEMMA: Is it wrong to hide the 'a' cards from Tim, Lord? Maybe they are Your way of prompting Tim and I'm holding You back? What if someone had tidied away Gideon's fleece? Once, Tim left his Berghaus fleece outside overnight and it was wet in the morning (but only because it had rained).

Just tucking into some cheese and onion crisps. Must start diet when this family pack runs out.

7pm

Quite a big afternoon. Following definite spiritual prompting, popped to library to look for cookery books for the weekend. In spite of forgotten 'a', amazing meal for Tim still going ahead. All parking spaces right outside the library were taken, so quickly nipped into the disabled space (they're so nice and wide). Decided it was OK to park in one as I was only going to be a minute and trying to find somewhere for that amount of time would be completely legalistic—plus, am under grace not law. Once at door though, saw library wasn't open until 2pm, another twenty minutes. Phooey!

Decided couldn't stay reading Bible in disabled space (twenty minutes no longer legalistic, just plain wrong) and didn't want angry disabled person banging on my window, so drove up the road, parked on the main road and sat reading my Bible with big lorries rattling past. Prayed to be released from stronghold of wanting to park in disabled spaces, even for short periods. At what point does it go from being OK to not being OK? Two minutes? Five? Nine minutes, 43 seconds? Or is it just not

OK at all, which seems a bit excessive when no other space is free?

At 2 o'clock, went back—disabled spot was still the only one that was free—so parked in nearby supermarket car park to avoid moral confusion. True I wasn't going there to shop, but as I've shopped there so many times in my life when I never had a car, decided it was fine.

Pinned a personal ad on the community board advertising artistic services—portraits, murals, still lives and tuition. Then got a Masterchef book out of the library—recipes from previous contestants—with some others thrown in from more established chefs. All the recipes in the book are sufficiently complicated to make (I can't be doing easy anymore). Recipes need to be multi-process, use *all* the hobs on the cooker, along with both ovens, the fridge and freezer, at least five gadgets and have a very high likelihood of giving me a nervous breakdown before I'm even *willing* to consider making them. I do however, draw the line at Michel Roux Junior's recipe for a three-tiered sesame seed biscuit stack with peeled grapes in between each layer and tiny pipings of cream. Who in their right mind would make this Lord? You may as well give someone a packet of golden syrup sesame snaps, a bunch of grapes and some squirty fresh cream—job done.

POINT OF OBEDIENCE TO REMEMBER: Tim says must never make him anything with cardamom in it. The occasional pod hidden in a curry is fine. But not say, cardamom ice-cream or cardamom bread. Me, I draw the line at pears in desserts (too bland and grainy). For me, puddings have to have carbohydrate in them and be served with cream or custard.

TOTALLY POINTLESS THING: I often drive myself insane by looking up the page number for a recipe in the index, then forget it about a second later and have to look it up all over again. Perhaps a vaguely fun but largely pointless exercise would be playing 'guess the page' all by myself? I could guess and guess and guess away, until I guessed correctly.

Also popped into M&S to buy some sticky rice to go with tonight's duck. Had a browse in Indigo and the Limited range (don't do Per Una, the swirling colours and frills give me a headache). Accidentally nudged a mannequin and apologized profusely, thinking it was a person. Then tidied up a few items (hate seeing clothes on the floor) and alerted shop assistant to a garment being on the wrong sized hanger. (Good citizen not entirely relevant to being an obedient wife but nonetheless connected).

Clothes-browsing done, went to the food section: bliss. All the day's stresses melted away and I lost myself in gazing at poshly-packed items such as Italian biscuits that some poor old Tuscan granny has made for decades with her arthritic, weathered hands. Part of the joy of gliding around M&S food heaven is the ease with which their trolleys move—they're simply the best. They're not too big or too low and very rarely do they have a malfunctioning wheel.

Hunted out the duvet-clad-because-of-the-fridges assistants, who have those yellow sticker guns they use for marking up reduced items. I follow them around like an albatross follows a fishing trawler. Brought to mind that verse from Matthew 24, 'Where there is a dead body, the vultures will gather'. Never really known what that verse means but I can bet my bottom dollar Jesus wasn't talking about loitering around M&S food counters, waiting for discounts. In the end, I pounced on some reduced fish fillets, burgers and some deli food.

After spending £70 when thought would only spend £3, had a hot chocolate in the cafe and a slice of their Victoria sponge. It's a three-tiered creation and twice the size of an ordinary one. Got my loyalty card stamped which made me feel organised and I found nice spot down the side to sit in (had to move twice, once to avoid a screaming child, then a second time to avoid a woman on her phone).

Also observed several people sit down to reserve a seat before they bought their produce. *There should be a law against this Lord.*

It's just so unfair on people who have queued and find themselves wandering around with a tray of hot drink and nowhere to sit!

Enjoyed my hot chocolate, my cake and that tiny cookie they give you. I even leant over to the next table to take someone else's. The person had gone, I should add, I didn't just lean over and steal it when they weren't looking. Imagine if I were so desperate that I did that and got caught? Lately, I've been giving the till assistant 'give-me-two-cookie-eyes' and I've even said, 'I really, really love these little cookies'—hoping they'll give me more. (It's worked only once, stingy things).

Perhaps I should give up being an artist and work at Marks and Spencer? I think I'd find it really satisfying. I don't know if I'd pass the interview they do, only thing. Isn't it the retail equivalent of joining the SAS?

THOUGHT BEFORE THE LORD: Sometimes I wonder, what if I just started to work for M&S unofficially, just by turning up and being useful? I could arrive everyday looking smart and start tidying clothes and answering people's queries. I could get away with it for a while at least. (Wouldn't get paid though, only thing, so bit of a dud idea).

At home, Gemma rang to see if I would consider doing a painting based on one of the photos from her wedding when it happens in September, for £50. I think she thought that was quite a good price, even though it will take me days and days and days and days. Have said yes, even though after tax and pre-tax tithe will mean am working for about 2p an hour. Tim walked past while I was on the phone to her, enabling me to take advantage of our forgotten 'a' brilliantly.

'Wonderful Gemma. Yes, I'd be honoured to paint something based on your *wedding*. What a *memorable day* your *wedding day* will be. I'm sure you and Kieran will *never forget* the date you *got married* and a painting will help you remember your *wedding* every year, won't it?'

Tim gave me a funny look and then he went to play with Pluto in the lounge with a squeaky toy. Why-o-why do they always get the noisiest toy out when I'm on the phone? I'm sure it's a subconscious attempt at getting my attention.

Gemma also said they're fundraising at church for a new boiler. She gets to know all these things before anyone else with working in the office now. She and Kieran are planning a sponsored swim in matching swimwear.

Feel like running a fundraising event for ourselves, frankly. 'Sponsor Tim and Emily to go on holiday, as they've not been on one for ages'.

Bad thing: Not done much painting, probably because of resentment over 'a' and because of disabled parking turmoil at library when ended up in Tesco's. I actually tried to ring that particular branch of Tesco to repent and say I'll never park there again if I'm not shopping there too—but could I find a local number anywhere? In end, said sorry to someone in customer services in another part of the country, then hung up.

Tim is chasing Reg around the lounge too now, not just Pluto. He makes life look so easy and has no idea about the problems I face (parking worries, freezer charts, panto horses and the major question of where dead moths end up). Oh, and not painting.

Good thing: Have found an amazing App called Find Friends—it lets me track Tim's whereabouts at any time and lets me time meals to the second he walks in. How many other wives are doing this around the country, I wonder? Probably none! (O.R. 1,000).

Other bad thing: Experimented with some eye makeup I've had for ages but never used—pale grey, dark grey and white. Asked Tim if I looked like a panda bear and he said no— without even looking up! THIS OBEDIENCE AND

MAKING AN EFFORT BUSINESS IS GETTING ME NOWHERE LORD.

QUESTION BEFORE THE LORD: I cannot get Darlene Zschech's Here I Am Send Me out of my head. Do singers ever get their own songs on their brain and wish they hadn't written them? I bet they do.

Thursday 19 August

12pm

Tim got up before me this morning, full of the joy of the Lord. It's not surprisingly really, given I've been such an amazing wife all week. Felt envious he was on the other end of the emotional spectrum to me (painting going dreadfully and am still bitter re anniversary). He didn't ask why I was glum, he just asked if he was having a cooked breakfast again. When I said, 'No,' he didn't look devastated as I hoped he would. He said, 'Just as well, I don't want to put on weight'.

He then left for work with a banana and one of his strange cycling bars that look like something astronauts take into space, singing Matt Redman's 10,000 Reasons For My Heart to Sing.

PLEASE LORD, HELP ME TO PAINT SOMETHING BEFORE I GO CRAZY.

Had a pray, then went straight to my easel. Obliterated my panto horse of the apocalypse in a few dramatic moves and ended up with an awful, oily, grey brown mass, all over the canvas. Pluto came in, took one look, whimpered, then went out.

Friday 20 August

1pm

Tried to do a bit more on the bowl of fruit, but Tim has taken the banana that was there to work (last one of the bunch), ruining my composition. What am I meant to do now, Lord?

Felt led to have another mini-cathartic clear-out, this time of Tim's junk area at the bottom of the wardrobe. Mid-rummage, found his old, pale blue, suede slip-ons with square toes that he used to wear all the time and which I really despise. I hid them shortly after we got married, replacing them with some light blue Crocs which he now also wears all the time. I wonder what Man did before Crocs were invented, Lord? I too wear Crocs all the time and totally love them (they're practically as useful as my actual feet).

As I held his slippers in my hands, I knew that the godly thing to do would be to confess to Tim that I hid them all those years ago, reinstate them, and give him the final say on what he wants to do with then.

I might have done that before Lord, but given he's forgotten a date that should be engraved on his memory, he can lump his slippers, I'm going to throw them away! They're so awful Lord, You probably hate them too! I recently threw out a pair of square-toed boots of mine, so it's not as if am not practising what am preaching, is it?

1.10pm

Offending slippers gone. Lobbed them into the wheelie bin and slammed shut the lid. Hurray! Feel purified, purged and liberated. Have thrown pile of potato peelings on top, plus a plastic lamb chopper, so they're *totally hidden.*

6pm

Tim home and tired after a hard day's work. Has gone to lie on the sofa with Pluto and Reg. Am starting to feel guilty re what I've done Lord (chucking out his You-know-what's). Been out to bin to have a quick look—it pongs really badly.

6.15pm

Tim asked me how my work was going and said that he's been praying for me.

Feel even worse now. O. R. minus a million.

Bad thing: Odd-sock-charger-storage-system (OSCSS) has failed. Tim has taken one of his storage socks to re-unite it with a recently retrieved original, therefore meaning he has a charger on the loose again. Need to either find another odd sock for the system to work (not ideal), or, find another system (not ideal either).

QUESTION BEFORE THE LORD: Maybe I should buy some socks especially for this purpose?

ANSWER FROM THE LORD: That would be ridiculous.

Saturday 21 August

10am

Tim has not forgotten our anniversary after all! He said he thought that *I'd* forgotten, or that I wasn't that bothered (as if!). He said he'd seen the cards in the kitchen table drawer and thought I was so 'not bothered' that I'd put them away without even opening them. Day out cycling with the lads totally cancellable and he only agreed to it when he thought I didn't care. What a relief!

We've released one another from the bondage of a) rushing out to buy one another a card and thereby saving a small fortune (cards are so expensive these days) and b) we've spared ourselves from the hassle of spending hours painting/drawing one in an attempt to create a personalised card that shows our love goes beyond shop-bought ones.

Tim wants us to go for a long country walk this afternoon but I reminded him I can't. I have a doctor's appointment coming up about my suspected flat foot (to be honest, don't know how he's forgotten given am hobbling around more than Gandalf out of Lord of the Rings).*

*THOUGHT BEFORE THE LORD: How our bodies work is so weird, Lord. I'm so glad You put all our vital organs and veins on the inside. Because if they were on the outside, we'd not only look frightful, it would be really bloody and messy too and we'd pick up an awful lot of dirt and dust on the way (hair, sweet wrappers, bus tickets, paperclips, grit, buttons, peelings and that's just for starters). You might also lose vital organs as you traipsed around, although operations would be easier, as it would all be easy access. I can't wait to get to heaven and have my heavenly body, Lord. I hope I can fly, speak hundreds of languages, play the harp and be a size 10. I'd also love to be good at sport for once in my life.

Told him to go out on his bike and let me get started on tonight's fancy meal—sea trout for starter, halibut and crayfish for main and for pudding, chocolate fondants with Chantilly cream. He's over the moon.

Tomorrow we're eating out at this place that does the most amazing chips. Basically, I'm going to look at what's served with chips and just pick that. I might even have chips with chips.

Bad thing: Foot really hurts after every work out now. What do I do Lord, stop going? I only joined because I didn't want to look like a 39-year-old pork pie anymore. I filled in the health questionnaire, got into some gym gear which I'd cobbled together, then went for my induction. 'What do you want to achieve?' asked the instructor. 'I want to look like Angelina Jolie,' I said, for a joke. Slightly miffed that he roared with laughter and slapped his thigh quite so much, he then proceeded to set up some programmes, starting me off on level 1. LEVEL 1? He might as well have said, 'Look, just give up now love, and go back to your sofa'. As he talked me through what to do, music blared out of some speakers that were joined to a main stalk in the centre of the ceiling. There were four TV sets with different channels you could tune into with headphones if you wanted. TV1 was some kind of music video channel with scantily clad woman on it running around with guns (bound spirits of violence and impurity). The second was something like Bargain Hunt (bound spirits of gambling and covetousness), the third, a news channel (bound lawlessness, secularism and rebellion), and the fourth, football (felt nothing needed binding). None of them were for me I decided—I'd just listen to David Suchet reading the Bible, thank you very much. Looked sorrowfully at the channels and at last minute, bound spirits of idolatry for football.

Other bad thing: Think I eat more chocolate now go to the gym than ever before, justifying it with 'I must have burned off at least a million times more than this, so what's the problem?' Often after a work-out I guzzle two bags of Maltesers (all air anyway). Basically, if something is what I deem to be more than 50% air, I allow myself two.

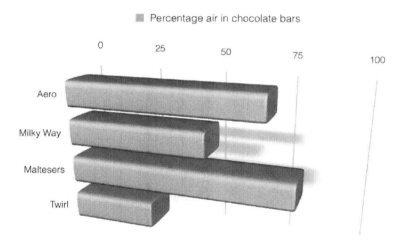

5pm

Good thing: After his cycle Tim drove into town to buy me an anniversary pressie (didn't even realise he'd gone!) While he was out, I fished his slippers out of the bin. They stank to high heaven so I've stuck them in the washing machine where they currently are thudding around on a delicate cycle with lots of detergent.

Bad thing: Tried to salvage brown oily mess on canvas by giving it a few decisive strokes in yellow and red. Showed it to Tim when he got back. He thinks it shows potential as a backdrop for something else. And there I was, thinking it was done! There's nothing like a spouse to tell you how it is, even on your anniversary.

Sunday 22 August

4pm

Lovely, lovely anniversary. Dinner a success and have advanced cooking skills 100% (O.R. 1000). Over breakfast before church, Tim spotted I was using the wider cereal bowls in a relaxed and posh kind of way and we went into the lounge to read out the Bible readings we had at our wedding: Psalm 139 (but not the violent bit at the end), Romans Chapter 12 about being living sacrifices and honouring one another above ourselves and Ecclesiastes Chapter 4, verses 9-12 about two being better than one. Ecclesiastes 4 is also the passage which also talks about one of you falling over and the other one being there to pick you up. Hand on heart, I can say we've not done this in our marriage once yet. Last winter, when I went flying on some ice outside church, Tim was at home with a cold and another time when Tim went flying on some mud in the park, I was in the park cafe toilet (I always seem to be on the toilet when major things happen).

In what was must have been a Holy Spirit-twist, Tim got to the slippers in the washing machine yesterday before I did.

'Where have these been?' he asked, delighted to have found them. 'Have you washed them especially for me, Em? I didn't know you could wash suede'.

'You can't,' I said. I had to come clean in the end and tell him everything. He was very gracious actually (I'd have been livid). (O.R. minus 100 at least, then minus another 100 for throwing them out in the first place).

Good thing: Tim not forgetting our 'a'; and having double chips at the restaurant (according to Isaiah Chapter 61, having a double portion is entirely biblical).

Bad thing: At restaurant, used disabled loo as was too full to go upstairs to the ordinary one. Yes, I feel I can now resist taking a disabled space outside the library Lord, but when faced with an empty disabled *loo* in my time of need, I seem to cave in. When I came out, a lady was there in a wheelchair, seething. Considered putting on a limp or saying had left my crutches at home but given they'd have been blatant lies, I took her rebuke on the chin and hoped she would never find out am a Christian, ever. (Actually, it probably did her good to wait).

Other good thing: Tim has bought me the most gorgeous necklace, a sort of sword type thing on a silverish chain to remind me of the sword of the Spirit verse in Ephesians. Will never be mean to him ever again.

Monday 23 August

Been stomping around and proclaiming scriptures about provision while trying to improve my End Times abstract. Someone who saw my ad on the community board rang. They thought I was a painter and decorator and were asking for a quote to do their house. I said sorry, but I was an artist, not a painter and decorator and that was the end of that.

Maybe though, I should ditch art, Lord and become a painter and decorator? Or maybe I have a hidden talent or skill that I haven't discovered, like painting and decorating. What if I'm good at archery or gymnastics or swimming but I just don't know it? Often, when I do aqua aerobics, I do really feel like

Jessica Ennis as I get into the pool—but when I start the class, the feeling goes.

Or, perhaps I'm good at woodwork, or accountancy, or maybe, I'm a really good Formula 1 racing driver but haven't found out? Maybe if Tim and I went to Silverstone, You would have me rise up and volunteer my services during some kind of critical moment when they needed an extra driver, but for some inexplicable reason, there was no one else around. I'd take up the challenge valiantly yet humbly, and amazingly, discover I was brilliant at it and win. I'd end up on the podium, in some kind of brand-laden cap and outfit, shaking champagne over everyone with an absurdly large sum of money being transferred into our bank account (which I'd tithe, *obviously*). Or, perhaps I'm a talented conductor and all I need is an orchestra to realise it? Or a harpist? Have always wanted to play the harp Lord, it's just knowing which strings to pluck, when and in what order. To think there could be a talent I haven't found out yet Lord, it breaks my heart! I don't want to get to heaven and have You say, 'Emily you were really good at Buckaroo but you never found out'.

I know, I've got it! Perhaps I should set up a Christian business selling something that churches use, like paper cups or office equipment? I could call it 'Charles Spurgeon Office Supplies' so that churches would immediately know that I was a Christian business—and thereby order lots of things for ever. If a non-Christian business wanted to buy something off me, they could too, of course. They'd ask me who Charles Spurgeon was and I'd tell them, thereby spreading the Gospel, reaching thousands.

I can't see myself selling photocopiers, only thing.

15 minutes later, after period of prayer, possible hidden talents the Lord is bringing to mind:

1) I'm good at squirting myself in the eye while eating a grapefruit. I haven't met anyone else who's good at this but it

happens to me at least twice a week (I eat a lot of grapefruit). In fact, I even squirted custard in my eye once (a dollop jumped out of the pan as I was heating it). What are the chances of that happening Lord, probably a trillion to one!

2) I'm also good at fitting things into the fridge freezer, no matter how impossible it looks. This is actually very useful, arguably more useful than Formula 1 racing, although not as well paid (not paid at all actually). There's nothing worse than having a packet of peas you can't fit in the drawer, or bread, or mince. (Sometimes, I have to do a full unload followed by a full re-load and believe me, that takes skill).

3) I'm good at making crumble and enjoy giving it away. I also often provide people with a tin of custard too. In fact, one of my dreams would be to get a space rocket, fill it with crumble, take off and fly above the Earth, then pull a switch and dump it over the planet so everyone could have some, birds and animals included. Sometimes I wonder if I force my crumble on people though Lord, and I give it to them whether they want it or not.

Bad thing: When I stepped on the scales this morning, found had put on 4lb. Kicked scales about a bit but no change. How can that be, after only a day or two of slight indulgence? Now I know how You feel Lord, hating dishonest scales.

Noon

Went for a swim to work off yesterday's chips which was followed by crème brûlée for pudding (I love crème brûlée. It's my top fave pudding—along with crumble, sticky toffee pudding, jam roly poly, cheesecake, trifle, profiteroles, lemon tart with a quenelle of cream, Bakewell tart (also with a quenelle of cream), rice pudding, brownies, lemon meringue, anything with salted caramel, Victoria sponge, Eton mess, vanilla slices, baked Alaska, chocolate fondants, Manchester tart, crêpes Suzettes, banoffee pie and anything frangipane).

Had a pray, asking God to help me paint/find work/lose weight, then went to the pool, as God helps those who help themselves. I got into my usual lane (the fast one) that's cordoned off from the general swimming area where people who insist on talking go. (Wondered briefly if I should train to be a fitness instructor and not an artist, but can't really see myself in a leotard, firing out orders).

I was swimming away like I always do, when out of nowhere, the lifeguard (who knows me), flagged me down and asked me to leave the fast lane and move to where the talkers were. I could not believe it! True, the only other person in my lane was a guy who kept nearly mowing me down, but I am pretty fast most of the time (well fast-ish—medium on a good day anyway—OK then, probably not fast enough to swim in the fast lane, *ever*).

'Would you mind moving out of this lane please love?' he said, 'I don't want you to get caught by that chap'. I took my goggles off even though I'd heard him perfectly well, as I wanted him to tell me straight to my face and not to a piece of plastic held on by a strap. He may as well have said, 'Look love, you're going so slowly, you're nearly going backwards'.

Deeply offended, I moved to the part of the pool with no lanes, thinking if I ever needed a sign not to be an instructor, it was this—I could never be this brutal or confrontational. Feeling really bitter, I then nearly collided with two women doing breast stroke side by side and talking while I was trying to do crawl. Made sure I swam *as fast as I could* so that the lifeguard would see I wasn't slow and definitely fast enough for the fast lane. Dare I admit it, I even toyed with the idea of bumping into one of the women on purpose—not in a dangerous way or anything—just a little bump, so the chap could see the error of his ways. Just as I kept telling myself it was highlighting the pride in my character that God obviously wanted be rooted out, the fast man left.

'What now?' I thought. The fast lane is empty but here I am, hemmed in by women doing breast stroke side by side and talking.

All I'd gone for was a quiet swim Lord, but now it had become a quest to prove I wasn't slow (even though I am). Pretended to glance casually at some kids who nearly drowned me with a wave of water as they jumped in right next to me—then some bright spark guy with a huge crucifix tattoo on one arm and a serpent on the other (internal spiritual battle or what) came in and started doing butterfly, practically emptying the pool of water with every stroke!

Bound all rebellion then left exhausted, picking up a empty shampoo bottle that someone had carelessly dropped and an empty crisp bag. I then bumped into Gemma who was just arriving for her swim with Kieran. Probably swimming side by side in their matching underwear and talking if I know them.

First good thing: Doing 40 lengths (chip/crème brûlée guilt fading away).

Second good thing: Swimming incident showed me that sin lurks in the most unexpected of places, even pools. Have forgiven the lifeguard and repented of pride and judgement.

Third good thing: Tim requested chopped fruit in his artisan, bespoke and prayed over packed lunches. Have done cubed apple and pears like a shot (O.R. 10/10). He is so blessed to have me.

And finally: Paul and Mandi are coming this weekend. Am praying they will come to church on the Sunday and that dinner—spatchcocked quails, followed by lamb shoulder with roast pots and choccy fondants for pud—will be a triumph!

Off to see doc.

4pm

Been to doc's re suspected flat foot. To make it worth her while, gave her a potted history of twenty years of back trouble and that there is also the distinct possibility that one leg is shorter than the other.

She asked to have a look at my foot and so I lifted it up and swung it towards her (bit embarrassing really, as my tights have a hole in the toe area). She prodded it until I yelled and suggested that perhaps I had early arthritis. Rubbish, I thought, and bound this negative proclamation, am only 39. She then discounted that theory (battle won in heavenlies) and suggested an insole to which I said, 'Won't that just treat the symptom, and not the *cause*?'

Gave her the example of the Leaning Tower of Pisa to show her what I meant. I said, 'To fix the tower, would the Italians give it a prop, or would they go about correcting its foundations?' To which she replied that the Italians probably wouldn't want to fix their leaning tower as the lean is what makes it a tourist attraction in the first place (still, she got my point).

In the end, I accepted the offer of a podiatry appointment (pictured someone brainy in a white coat analysing my gait) in the next few months. She also said to exercise but not overdo it (fine by me).

As I left, I felt had to say something about the power of prayer and being a Christian and that if my foot got healed through prayer, I'd cancel the podiatry appointment so as not to waste NHS time (which to be honest, felt had done anyway). Also offered her a family portrait half price—she said she'd think about it—then went back to her screen.

Clicked door shut and went.

Tuesday 24 August

It's my turn to make a cake for home group tonight. With the verse 'do unto others as you would have them do unto you' ringing in my ears, am planning to make a large, multi-layer Victoria Sponge (because that, Lord, is what I hope others will bake for me).

I'm going to have to put it into one of those huge Tupperwares where the lid is the main container and the flat lid is the base. The other week, Tim asked me why all our Tupperwares have our name on them. I said, 'It's because I know what Tupperware is like in church circles—once it leaves your house, you have to accept you may never see it again ever again'.

All over the world right now, Tupperware tubs are being passed around from one Christian woman to another, with a train of cakes, stews and lasagnes in them in constant orbit. I don't think it's because Tupperware brings out a criminal edge in people, quite the contrary—it's based on the Christian assumption of trust that one day, your Tupperware will find its way safely back into your loving arms. If it doesn't, you will probably acquire someone else's quite by accident, and as it's only Tupperware, it doesn't really matter (true in the light of eternity, but not in the light of one's everyday baking needs).

I know how it happens too. You lend your Tupperware to someone and then the person you've lent it to decides to lend it to someone else, justifying it by saying, 'I'm sure Emily won't mind you having it, but just make sure you give it back to her and not me, OK?' Then the new person says, 'Oh Emily, I know her! Of course I'll give it back to her'. But they never do.

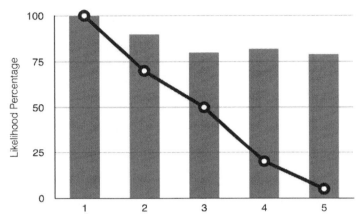

○ Likelihood of unlabelled Tupperware being returned
■ Likelihood of labelled Tupperware being returned

You had quite a good chance of getting your Tupperware back off Person No. 1, but now the chain is longer, it's much less likely. Your tub's nomadic pilgrimage through Christian homes has now begun and unless you have a label with your name on it to prick the person's conscience, it's probably curtains.

NB: I had a Tupperware end up by the Sea of Galilee once. This is because I once gave some cake in it to someone at church, thinking I'd get it back the following week. I had nothing for ages (plus it was labelled) and the next time I saw it, it was on Facebook in a photo in Israel (with my sticker and name on the side and everything, albeit faded). The person had taken it on holiday *with her*, Lord. At the point when I clapped eyes on it, it had some kind of tomato and feta salad in it with onions and black olives which if I'm honest, looked a bit old and wilted, but it would have been hot out there so it was pretty understandable. I have never seen my Tupperware ever again and it was one of my favourites. For all I know, it could have been left on some bench somewhere and is currently being used by a family in the Gaza strip or by a Rabbi for falafel.

One day, I might engrave my name on my Tupperwares using a safety pin, if I ever have the time.

3pm

Making this Victoria sponge is more work than I thought. Am listening to a sermon about how when you become a Christian, the Ten Commandments become promises, not rules.

I've got just enough eggs, PTL. The amount of times I've been caught out with a shortage of eggs Lord, it's absolutely staggering—I always have to rely on the goodness of a neighbour.

Eggs are strange things, when all is said and done. I rarely have hard boiled eggs, as I hate the thought of boiling an egg and cracking it open, only to find a completely cooked chick. And to think I could just dig in with my spoon and end up with a mouth full of soggy feathers! I don't like the way they roll around wonkily either. Life's unpredictable enough.

4pm

While whisking the butter and sugar together and adding the eggs one a time, I sprayed myself with gunk, while also getting it on my top and my face. Why didn't I just go to Mark's and get a cake there, Lord? I have no idea where I get this stupid idea—to make everything from scratch. Since getting married, I have made pots and pots of jam, dozens if not hundreds of crumbles (have overactive rhubarb patch) and have chutney literally pouring out of my ears.

POINT BEFORE THE LORD: One day I'd like to 'go one back' and make my own butter. Apparently, if you whisk double cream for ages, that's what you get. Actually I could go back *even further* than that and buy my own goat/cow. I think it would have to be a goat though, as cows are too big.

In fact, I think goats should be used on lawns instead of mowers because:

a) No electricity is used

b) No mowing is needed

c) As the grass is cut, the goat is fed and the owner gets organic fresh milk, so everyone is happy

d) You have rather an original and spritely pet

e) If you trained it, you could potentially end up with a guard-goat.

SOUL-SEARCHING QUESTION, LORD: In making this cake, am I being a Martha—or do I mean Mary? I can never remember which is which, which sort of says it all. Spending time being busy but not spending it with You. Anyway. Best go. Need to cut out greaseproof liners for my tins as those shop bought ones never fit. Also have primeval urge to do some hand-washing—not dissimilar to Pluto wanting to bury a bone.

9.45pm

Very bad thing: Just back from home group. Took my Victoria sponge, which was a total triumph. Initially, not a single person commented on it (i.e. got no praise) but what was about a 1,000 times worse was that I didn't even get a piece. I was so busy praying for Doris's arthritis to be healed in the other room (and her for my art and my foot) that by the time we got back, everyone was merrily tucking into the final remnants of their giant Tim-cut pieces, licking their lips, and nothing—not even a crumb—was left for me. Glared at Tim whose eyes said an innocent, 'What?' and then I said that, 'You've 'muzzled the ox'.' I, the hard-working bakeress, had got zilch, to which he replied, 'The last will be first and the first will be last'. I said I didn't know that scripture applied to cake. Does that mean when I get to heaven I'm going to get a giant piece of cake to make up for all the cake I've missed out on on earth? Will I live inside a cake, or have a room made out of sponge? He always throws the last will be first scripture at me when I least expect/deserve it and what can I say back. Surely my muzzled ox scripture overrides his? Next time, if there is a next time, I'm going to be the one who cuts up the cake, not him, and if I'm called away, I'll take a piece with me. Ideally, I will not pray until after cake has been consumed, unless it's an emergency. (O.R. irrelevant Lord, as this is about justice and not obedience).

Other bad thing: To cap it all, according to synthetic-muffin-Pauline, I have been making tea incorrectly all my life. The key is to use freshly boiled water (never re-boiled water which is poisonous apparently), to warm the cup first (not just whip a cold one out of the cupboard) and to scald the teabag to death for two minutes, no less. *Under no circumstances must milk be added before the water or before the bag is taken out.* I've always known I've been going wrong somewhere in life Lord, and now I know what it is. I've *often* added the milk when the bag's still in it too, and dare I admit it, I've sometimes added milk to the water before the teabag. I probably made my first cup of tea at around the age of seven. As I'm 39 now, that means I have been making tea wrong for around thirty-two years. At around three cups a day, that's 365 x 3 = 1095 cups of rubbish tea a year. Over 32 years (my estimated tea-making life) that's a grand total of 1095 x 32 = 35,040 dud cups (will add 24 more to make up for leap years). So, having never warmed the cup or timed the steep, I can honestly say that the last 35,064 cups of tea I have made before have been substandard. How am I meant to be an obedient wife if I can't even make tea, Lord? And am I really expected to not have a piece of my own cake?

QUESTION BEFORE THE LORD: I wonder what cakes You had when You were on earth. Some kind of thing with dates and honey in it maybe, with the odd pounded up locust for crunch and texture? There's no way I could have coped with just one very basic cake.

Yet another bad thing: Theme at tonight's home group was forgiveness. Was there anyone we needed to forgive, Stuart & Liz asked (as if admitting to that would be easy in public). A person, God, or ourselves? If we don't forgive, we won't be forgiven, and also, unforgiveness distances us from God as it creates a barrier and hardens our hearts. There was a long silence. I brought up the Tupperware in Israel as a sort of light-hearted example, but which if I think about it enough, still hits a nerve (although of course now I have Tim to forgive re the cake and Pauline re the tea too—where does it all end Lord?) Liz said forgiveness starts with a decision and not a feeling, as we may never feel we want to forgive. She said forgiveness isn't saying that someone's sin against us doesn't matter either—it's just taking them off our peg and putting them on God's to deal with in the right way at the right time. He is the just judge and it starts to free us from anger and bitterness and pain. Said I knew forgiveness was key but that forgiveness is also really perplexing and strange. Why does it even exist? Why not just seethe forever, or take revenge, or leave it at that, and go off in a huff, forever breaking off the relationship with whoever's hurt you? Guess God could have just folded His arms and decided He wasn't going to forgive us, meaning Jesus would have never needed to set foot on this planet and die a horrible death. There can be no forgiveness without the shedding of blood i.e. a death, it says in the Bible, and that's what we all really need in this life, forgiveness, as we always fall short sooner or later, not matter how 'nice' we are. It's the relationship with the Father that Adam and Eve broke through their sin that needs restoring and only sinless Jesus's death is the perfect, cover all sacrifice for us, both now and forever more. I suppose if we don't forgive, not only are we not forgiven ourselves—thereby coming under judgement—it's also pain and broken relationships all the way—a grave for us and a grave for those who've hurt us. All too often Lord, it seems that if someone hurts you, if you don't forgive them, you end up being at fault (guess that's the paradox of Christianity).

Good thing: On way home, Tim apologised about me not getting any cake. He just didn't want me to feel guilty about the calories afterwards. I said that by an act of the will I forgave him (didn't want to though).

Wednesday 25 August

Noon

Tried being a really disobedient wife all morning to see where it would get me (nowhere). Also thought that being a bit of a rebel might jolt me out of this creative impasse (it hasn't). Got up late, didn't do any pots, didn't hoover or iron and watched daytime TV for an hour and a half. Didn't pick up Tim's used tissues and socks off the floor either (really wanted to, but resisted). Then I ate lots of chocolate, had two extra coffees resulting in a major caffeine high and put all of Tim's T-shirts (un-ironed) into his drawer (he wears them under his fleeces anyway so what's the point?)

After that, I went online to browse for new clothes and see what ready meals Waitrose has.

I loved doing nothing if I'm honest but I did feel sullied by daytime TV and all those scary ads about debt, gambling and life insurance.

Counteracted the situation by getting Paul and Mandi's room ready for the weekend. I wonder where they're going on their holidays this year? They have about ten every year.

Bound and repented of envy, then prayed in the Spirit and added some finishing touches to my new vegetable still life (not very good).

Then popped to M&S to get some nibbles for P&M as they like to graze on things before a meal (don't know how they do it and still stay so skinny). I wish M&S would make pairs of blinkers available for customers wanting to go in and not impulse-buy a thousand extra items (it'll never happen though, business suicide). Tried the thing of going round with just a basket. Didn't work. Filled my basket in about two minutes. When it became too heavy to carry, left it at the end of an aisle, then darted around the shop for things like a lunatic. From a distance, I saw a man knock into my basket. He hit his shin on the metal rim, then he hopped about and looked around for someone to blame. Scared he might sue me for shin damage, I pretended it wasn't mine. Stared at a prawn curry for ages, then at him from the corner of my eye, then when he finally gave up and left, I went and whipped my basket away. Should I have gone up to him and apologized Lord? I guess I'll never know.

Also popped into TK Maxx for the first time ever. What a place. No wonder people leave there looking crazy. What happened to me as soon as I walked in? Found a gorgeous cardi right under my nose. £19.99 down from £45, blue with goldfinches all over it.

POINT BEFORE THE LORD: I think that if you're slightly unhinged you shouldn't go to TK Maxx because if you do, your judgement will crumble and you will start making strange choices very quickly. You'll start looking through the shoe department and replacing thoughts such as, 'They're awful' with 'They're really interesting'. Take me. I'm not *remotely* unhinged and yet I tried on a pair of golden cowboy boots and nearly ended up buying them. In order to get the boots out of my system, I found something else to distract myself with: a red Lycra top that I thought I'd try on. The changing room attendant had bright blue hair—thankfully that acted as another distraction—and I found that, very quickly, I fell out of love with the golden boots and the red top too (should have tipped her really, she saved me a small fortune). Given I was already in the changing room, I thought I'd try the red Lycra top on anyway, just to see how the goldfinch cardi looked with something on underneath it. Once in the cubicle, which you'd think was pretty safe, I proceeded to nearly kill myself pulling the red Lycra top over my head—the opening was too small. Top finally on, I concluded I looked like a malformed tomato.

As I started to take it off—it got stuck around my chin and I thought, oh no, I'm going to die trying to get this top over my head, it will not come off! Blue-haired girl will come in and find me, in here, dead. Tim will have to be informed that his wife was found asphyxiated in a red Lycra top in a changing room in TK Maxx and he'll forever not know whether it was an accident or suicide. The memorial service will be full of people not sure whether to laugh or cry, and also thinking what bad taste I had, trying on a red Lycra top, clearly too small, with a blue goldfinch cardi over it and a pair of golden cowboy boots too…

When got home, took Tim's T-shirts out of the drawer and ironed them after all.

1.15pm

Wrote this email.

Dear Manager at TK Maxx

Today I went into your wonderful grotto of a store and soon became lost in retail, not knowing where to go or who I even was anymore.

Now in the safety of my own four walls again, I have come up with some ways your customers can keep it together while shopping in your store.

They are as follows:

3 TOP TIPS ON HOW YOUR CUSTOMERS CAN STAY SANE

a) Customers need to stay focused. They shouldn't amble around everywhere i.e. they shouldn't look at children's clothes if they don't have children and/or at candles if they have no intention of burning a candle in their whole lives. They should time themselves on every visit, setting say, twenty minutes on their phone stopwatch. I know you will want them to stay in there for hours, but that's short term thinking. (If they go mad, they'll never return. This way, at least they might come back).

b) Ideally, customers should take a large boxing glove into the store with them (brought from your store potentially) and when they start feeling feverish, knock themselves out with it.

c) Finally, why not employ a Shakespearean fool type character like the one in King Lear, who speaks the truth to people about the strange things they try on in the changing rooms? People can take brutal honesty if given in right way and by the right person. Personally, I would love to be advised by a jester in a high street store.

I hope you find this useful.

Yours sincerely

Emily King

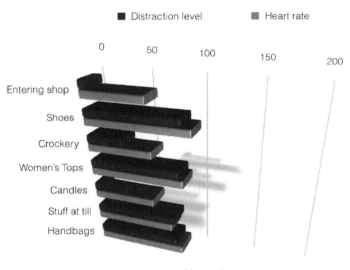

TK Maxx, heart rate and distraction levels on a regular shop (heart rate peaking most in shoe department)

■ Distraction level   ■ Heart rate

Heart rate

Bad thing: I rang Tim from the upstairs loo to request a cup of tea. Tried to mask fact was in loo with occasional cough but he saw right through it and hung up.

AREA OF GROWTH: Think I'm becoming more gracious Lord. When I asked Tim if he could tell anything different about his lovely clean keyboard and mouse that I Dettol-ed last night and he said no he couldn't, I didn't tell him so as not to lose out on my heavenly reward. (O. R. around 2,000).

Thursday 26 August

8pm

Just when I thought I was doing really well, am finding it really hard not to get cross Lord, when Tim disappears when I call dinner.

'Dinner's ready!' I yell, all hot and bothered, juggling plates, pans and ten thousand spatulas. He comes through briefly, then does his trick—vanishing—just like that. I know where he's gone—the loo—*but can't he go sooner?* I've done all the tricks—I've tried calling dinner five minutes early, which worked for a while, but then he worked out I was calling early and wouldn't come out till later with the trip to the loo still included.

Am seriously considering phoning up a security firm and asking how much it costs to install some kind of lock-down system that triggers shutters to roll down over the loo door downstairs and bathroom door upstairs when dinner is called.

What do I do Lord? Wait patiently? I can't! Start without him? That would just make me look annoyed (which I am). Or… should I hang a no entry sign on the loo door handle when dinner is being served and see how that goes down? At dinner time tonight, I called, 'Dinner's ready' in a semi-urgent yet hopefully-friendly tone, followed by, 'Can you serve up tonight hon?'—then I dived into the loo myself*.

*In all honesty, I didn't need the loo Lord, I just stood in there with my ear pressed to the door, listening to what would happen. Hearing Tim come into the kitchen and serving up, I then left the loo (flushing it to look as if I'd used it, however to make sure it wasn't a lie, I threw some bleach down it to clean it). Tim only went in as soon as I came out! I couldn't say anything, as I'd just been in myself! Aaaagggghhh!!!

WISE MOMENT: Am going to seek Christian counsel and ring Liz to see what she does.

10 minutes later

I knew it. Liz says Stuart is always around to help her with dinner. However, she also said there are more important things in a relationship than being in time for a meal. I said we'd have to agree to disagree on that one as I don't think there are. It's these little things, all stringed up, that make up your relationship—which is why they should be right. I don't like it Lord when there are no clear solutions.

Good thing: Have overcome feeling peeved re dinner and have made Tim his favourite packed lunch for tomorrow—fish fingers with lettuce and brown sauce on springy white bloomer (spring-back element essential, O.R. 10). Have to say, have upped my game with his packed lunches which are now 100% organic and locally-sourced (i.e. not-just-prayed-over-and-artisan). Have also invested in a new fleet of non-leeching, high quality, food safe Tupperwares from Lakeland that are for his packed lunches alone (will not be used at church, ever). Am also wrapping all sandwiches/baps in greaseproof paper. Hope he doesn't leave is P.L. behind, only thing (something else he's really good at, O.R. 2 for being critical). How quickly can good become tinged with bad, Lord! Love on the one hard, irritation on the other.

Friday 27 August

2pm

Tried a new gym class this lunchtime, Body Blast. 'How hard can it be?' I thought. It's the same instructor who does aqua and that's really easy. I can honestly say that it was *murder*. We used the step box for about half an hour but I couldn't follow the instructor's rapid orders and felt a total berk*.

*CORRECTION: Must not proclaim that am a berk—I am a Child of God. I was simply moving in a *berk-like way*.

I'm sure we defied the laws of physics at one point—I have never done a star jump so quickly in all my life. Every few minutes I asked the girl next to me what time it was. In the end she said in quite a firm way, 'The class lasts 45 minutes'. I shut up after that. What didn't help was that the instructor's iPad was malfunctioning. She'd taken it on holiday with her in the sun and now it was either playing the tracks too fast, or choosing tracks that were too fast in the first place. Some were so fast, they weren't music anymore—they were just one long note. There was a large amount of punching—punching left and punching right, punching up and punching down. I could have punched the instructor at one point.

In the end, I got pins and needles and thought I was going to die. To cap it all, my foot hurts too.

Bad thing: Just been into Tim's study with a 'there's no internet hon' expression on my face. I couldn't get onto any website, Lord. Thought he'd a) look up at me as soon as I walked in (he didn't) and b) spring into action when he heard me huff and puff (he didn't). In end had to say, 'Is your internet working hon? Because mine isn't,' with a tearful quiver in my voice. Then I stood around in a semi-tense way, expecting him to help (he didn't). 'My internet's fine,' he said. 'And can you stop all this huffing and puffing?' It's always the little things that trip me up.

Had a really weird lunch. Super Noodles with a Quorn peppered steak and a raw carrot.

Other weird lunches have had of late:

A bit of shredded cold roast lamb, again with raw carrot, and a sprinkling of couscous

Guacamole with two raw carrots (used carrots as utensils)

A baked potato with a poached egg, walnuts and cornichons

A Rachael's microwave rice pudding pot. If I leave it in the microwave too long, I lose about a fifth as it explodes onto the roof (at least I end up having a fifth fewer calories).

KAROLA WOODS

6pm

Hello Emily

Thank you for your email enquiring about working for TK Maxx.

Please register for jobs on our website where you will find all the latest opportunities.

Thank you for your interest.

Best wishes

Mr Ekuva Pane

Customer Services

TK Maxx

Job? I wasn't enquiring about a job! I was giving them crucial business feedback.

Just been to fill up on petrol and to check the air pressure and had a right game. Went to pay and get my air coupon and saw that the guy in front of me in the queue was getting his wallet out at around half a mile per hour while faffing around with various chocolate bars. When I heard him ask for an air coupon too I thought, oh no, he's going to get to the air pressure machine before me, and given his rate of doing things, I'll still be here by Christmas. Shot to other queue, paid like lightening and got my air coupon, then dived into car to get to the machine before him. Once there though, I couldn't find my coupon with the code on anywhere. Scoured pockets, seats, side door compartments—nothing.

Meanwhile, slow man was waiting patiently behind me. I became very demonstrative, looking for my coupon with big thrashing movements and lots of huffing and puffing to make it clear what was happening, all while flashing him an apologetic smile. In the end, had to move out of way to let him do his tyres first after all, and then go back in the kiosk to queue for another coupon. (The lady told me off actually, saying she shouldn't really be giving out more than one).

Why would those queue-jumping, rushing tactics have worked for someone else Lord, but not me? Any attempt to be first never seems to work for me. Is it because of that verse, the first will be last and the last first, working itself out in my life, yet again? Or is it because I'm a Christian and I should know better? When slow man finally left (he didn't take that long in the end), I did my tyres, and found my original coupon stuck beneath the pedals.

Maybe the godly thing to do would have been to offer to do the man's tyres for him in a servant-like fashion, like Jesus washing His disciples' feet (the tyres being the man's feet etc). I could have been a good witness Lord, instead I ended up sinning and looking mad.

Saturday 28 August

11am

Woke up with hair that looked like Pentecost was here. Was all coming together in a point like a flame at the top. For it to be shaped like that, I must have rotated in my sleep, as if on a spit.

Good thing: Think am finally making tea properly and Tim is starting to be able to tell the difference. Am scalding the cup and the teabag to death and waiting a whole two minutes before putting in the milk.

List of things am able to do during two minutes while tea brews:

Go to loo.

Put on a wash.

Send a few texts.

Plan tomorrow's meal and take something out of the freezer.

Do some exercises (won't be long before look like Angelina now).

Unstack/stack dishwasher.

Tweak online shop (risky as can take ages).

Throw together Tim's packed lunch (if have all artisan, organic, natural ingredients ready). Have started making *advanced* fruit salad for him actually, (although takes longer than two minutes). I aim for at least four fruits in a variety of styles: tropical, forest berries and traditional English garden.

Do Reg's cage—if he lets me near it.

Pray. Which should be number one!

5 minutes later

Paul and Mandi arriving later. Hope they come to church tomorrow but they probably won't.

'What do I need God for?' Paul said to Tim a few years ago. 'I've got Mandi, three cars, pots of money and I love what I do'. There's a lot you can say to a statement like that but it's hard to know where to start. I think Tim said something really unsubtle for him like,' Yes Paul, but where are you going to go when you die?' It sort of killed the conversation a bit, but sometimes, you have to open your mouth and say something, entrusting the consequences to God. Am making spatchcocked quail for the first time tonight. Have been wanting to spatchcock something for years (no idea why, I think I just like the word).

Bad thing: Reg has taken to calling 'dinner's ready' in my voice first thing in the morning, making Tim think I've finally lost it.

Annoying thing: White Golf man (WGM) has parked his car outside our house so there is nowhere for P&M to park when they arrive. He's doing this every weekend now and it's really annoying. There is plenty of room to park on his girlfriend's dad's massive drive over the road, but for some reason, he prefers to park outside our house, probably because he doesn't want to block the gangway for when his girlfriend's dad wants to take out his flash Porsch! Am praying for wisdom about the matter, but all I feel at the moment is rage. Yes we don't own the road, but isn't there an unwritten law in England about people not parking outside other people's houses?

2pm

Marital Newsflash

The mini-composter which has been the source of much marital discord in recent months is no more. Tim despised it as it was metal and it kept developing rust. In a concerted effort to sow peace into our relationship, I have replaced it with a large plastic Tupperware (mine, not one passing through our house on a Christian pilgrimage). Being plastic means it will never rust and marital discord surrounding this will be over, forever. (O.R. 5/10, as should have done it earlier).

POSSIBLE BUSINESS IDEA BEFORE THE LORD (SHUT DOOR IF WRONG LORD, FLING OPEN IF RIGHT): Maybe, I should set up a saffron or wasabi farm? Wasabi can't be that hard to grow, surely? Just looked it up. It's one of the hardest things to grow in the world as it's very, very fussy about its water and light. How about saffron? Saffron in Morrisons works out to be £10,000 a kilo but if I struck an exclusive supplier deal with them, I'm sure I could do it a bit cheaper. I quite like the idea of sitting around plucking stamen out of flowers all day. I could listen to David Suchet reading the Bible while interceding for the nations. I bet that's really hard to grow too.

5pm

P&M have arrived! It's so nice to see them. They have managed to park outside after all—WGM must have gone out somewhere. When he gets back, I hope it shows him that we need our space and that the only reason we don't use it is because he is there. Am getting on with dinner. Having watercress as a green, which I hope I don't regret as it's so multidirectional and hard to eat. Tim and P&M reading the papers in the lounge in a secular, middle class sort of way, drinking perfectly-made scalded-to-death tea in burning hot cups.

7.10pm

While monitoring the roast potatoes in the oven (stood and watched them turn golden as had nothing else to do) realised the heat coming out on the fan setting was drying my freshly-washed hair. Delighted was able to multitask just by standing still. Scrunched it a little as I stood there. Just hope don't smell of roast potatoes.

10.45pm

Am shattered Lord, while Tim and P&M still going strong (I wonder why!?) When-o-when will I learn, Lord? I always think entertaining's going to be fun, but by about half past nine, I want to either tell everyone to clear off or go to bed. I must have 'skivvy' written across my forehead in the spiritual realms Lord, and this isn't the first time that this has happened.

I remember once when we had some elderly friends over for New Year. I was practically in a coma by midnight, yet they were still going strong (probably because they'd done nothing but sit and eat all night while I worked my socks off). I even started making a hot water bottle under their noses and put on my pyjamas to give them a hint (it didn't work, they just thought I was making myself at home). '*I am at home!*' wanted to yell, but didn't.

P&M very complimentary about dinner but I thought the quails were awful. Wish I'd not bought them now, poor little things. The tiny amount of meat on them was like rubber and tasted of liver. The main was only slightly better. Did lamb shoulder from the Masterchef book—with copious amounts of seasoning—but which tasted of nothing. Where did I go wrong Lord? At least pudding was good. Chocolate fondants again, all gooey in the middle. At least could control how much

I had because some people are just so frugal (stingy) with portions.

We spoke about Masterchef quite a lot. Mandi likes the programme but doesn't like how John Torode and Greg Wallace have to eat and talk at the same time.

Asked them what colour they thought we should paint the lounge. They've told us to go out and get some tester pots, so that is what we're going to do. Am binding all spirits of magnolia as they've reigned in this house for far too long.

They're going on holiday to Brazil, followed by Paraguay, Argentina and Panama to round it all off.

Then we went to an old local we haven't been to for ages, The Three Bells. Went in our car so WGM couldn't get in P&M's space. P&M agree he shouldn't be there and that if they were in our shoes, they'd have said something by now. I said, 'Hear hear' but Tim says we can't stop him.

The Three Bells has been done out and totally ruined. Before, it was genuinely old. Now, it's been done out with new stuff that's trying to look old. Wallpaper that's a photo of stacked logs of wood, where as before, they had real logs.

In the car park, I spotted a huge Fiat based on the tiny Fiat from years ago. It looked like the original but on amphetamines. Mandi said people's cars are getting bigger and bigger. I said it was a reflection of society. People are seeking protection and security in big cars and things and thinking they're immortal. She said she thought I was right (I am). Unfortunately, I then remembered they've just got a new Audi A8.

Shocking thing: Not only did Tim go to the loo while I was serving up... P&M went too! When am I meant to go Lord, or is the chef meant to attach a colostomy bag to his/her apron strings?

Good thing: Reg very evangelical over dinner with no expletives whatsoever. Whether P&M come to church or not, they have definitely, definitely heard the gospel.

Sunday 29 August

4pm

Paul and Mandi have become Christians! We didn't even have to ask them to church, they came of their own accord! They received a thousand hellos (everyone has it drummed into them to greet newcomers) and they sat with me and Tim in the front row!

The sermon was all about everyone having a God-shaped hole in their hearts and the fact that no amount of money, relationships, success, drink or cars can ever fill it, just God alone. You can believe anything people tell you—but that it's only knowing Jesus and following His ways that really counts.

When the 'hands-up if you want to invite Jesus into your heart' request was made at the end, P&M put theirs up!

THANK YOU LORD!

All those years of prayer—just as I was beginning to think nothing would ever change, it has!

Feel I know what I'm going to paint now: Paul's conversion on the Road To Damascus—my painter's block has gone!

Monday 30 August

Noon

Am so elated re P&M, Lord. As a result, am on the crest of a Holy Spirit wave, painting well for the first time in months. Have started preparing preparatory sketches to prepare for the initial i.e. preparatory painting of St. Paul, falling off his horse as he's struck blind and brought to a knowledge of the Lord.

Maybe my oily mass earlier with the panto horse coming through was just a rumbling… and now my chains are gone?

I feel could evangelise to anyone right now—even Pat next door. She believes in God but not in all that 'Adam and Eve tosh' as she so often says. Shame, as if she did, it might help her come to terms with her biggest gripe: why suffering exists.

I know. I'll take the bull by the horns and go to explain it to her. It's about being bold Lord isn't it, and not missing any opportunity. I'll add that it was Adam and Eve's sin that broke their relationship with God who is holy and can't look at sin, and that their disobedience made them lose their authority and hand it to Satan instead. Tragically, thanks to them, we're all on the same gravy train in this life—until we choose to accept Jesus as our Savior and are made new in our spirits, in other words, until we're born again and have our relationship with God restored. The apple, Lord, the apple. Such a small ask, yet so big too. The apple was that awful moment in history when sin and evil entered the world—Adam and Eve chose to disobey Your simple command not to eat from the tree of good and evil—and the spiritual battle between good and evil began.

Pat blames God for the evil in the world and for the fallenness of Man when she should be blaming Satan! Can feel her resistance crumbling away in the spiritual realms right now— AM GOING ROUND IMMEDIATELY!

12.30pm

Pat not in. Will try later. (Holy Spirit really prompting me). Was rehearsing the line, 'It's only when we give our lives to Jesus that we're made new and can start again'... but will save it for later.

12.59pm

Pat out. Prompting still there though (I think.) Was going to say 'Jesus has done it all Pat, he's removed the dividing barrier' when she opened the door but she wasn't there!

1.30pm

Pat still not in. Prompting waning.

1.45pm

Pat not in. Prompting gone. I thought it was going to be my big chance Lord, and Pat's too.

2pm

Have carried on painting, while listening out for Pat coming back and my prompting returning. Have to say, just seen WGM park up outside and it's not even the weekend. Maybe I should go and evangelise to him instead? You love him as much as You love me Lord and I can't believe You died for him. There's no way I would have, he's far too selfish.

3.15pm

Wrestled with leaving an evangelical note on WGM's window screen but thought it was a tad excessive and insincere. Does insincerity matter though—surely it's Jesus preached that counts, and maybe it will be more powerful, given there isn't a bone within me that wants to go over? Have found a Nicky Gumbel 'Why Jesus?' booklet, but can't bring myself to put it under his wiper. Have just sat and glared at it.

4pm

In end wrote 'Please stop parking outside our house on the booklet' and left it under WGM's windscreen wiper.

Very pleased as combines kindness with firmness.

4.15pm

Have removed the booklet, thinking it's nuts and not a good witness.

Have torn off the top corner of booklet where I wrote my crazy message, but if I leave it on his car like that, all torn, will it look as if am leaving substandard tract? (Bet the early church never had these problems).

6pm

Went for a swim and swam in own bubble in slow lane, thinking about the world's reluctance to know Jesus, and my reluctance, fear or inability to go out to tell them. God hates cowardice, but knowing that somehow doesn't stop me from being cowardly. Why?

Bumped into Jane in the jacuzzi who was delighted that P&M put up their hands in the service and wanted to know all about it. She's joined a Christian-dating website and has got a date later this week. To think Lord, You knew all this would exist when You were here 2,000 years ago—computers, the web, cars, bicycles, nuclear weapons, the lot. I'm amazed You came to earth when You did. There's no way I'd have come to earth when there was no proper medicine, no electricity, no chocolate and no proper dentists. Asked Jane if she thought You ever got ill when You were on the earth. It doesn't say You did in the Bible, so maybe You didn't? Maybe You, human but not fallen, were disease-proof? You did touch a leper and didn't get leprosy, after all. Or maybe You weren't disease-proof, given You became man, but maybe You just didn't dwell on it, like we do. Jane said that when You were a boy, You must have fallen and grazed a knee when You were out playing football (whatever footballs were made of back then—compacted straw bound in sackcloth maybe?). Or, as a carpenter, You must have hit Your thumb with a hammer? And if You did get ill Lord, did You heal Yourself, receive crude medical treatment, pray to Your Father—or just wait for it to go? I guess this side of heaven, I'll never know.

Jane then went off to the sauna and I got out. In the changing room, while I was getting dressed, I went flying on the wet floor, on my poorly foot, which I could have easily broken. There are rules everywhere Lord about people getting dried by the showers and not by the lockers—it makes the floor slippery for everyone else. Seethed as watched several sopping-wet women dry themselves near me. 'Are you alright love?' one of them asked, seeing me in pain. 'No I'm not, because of people like you!' wanted to yell, but didn't. Instead, smiled sweetly and said, 'Thanks, I'm fine'.*

*Sometimes I wonder what life would be like if I was completely uncensored? Would I be more balanced or just a whole lot angrier? I bet Jesus didn't wonder what to do—He'd have known when to be lion and when to be lamb.

Jane entered the changing room, all red and hot from the sauna. I mentioned I'd gone flying and that I might put up some posters about the slippery floor. She thinks it's a great idea. She goes flying in the changing rooms at least once a week.

Tiny snagette: While my painting's going well, for the last half hour have been driven INSANE by a fly buzzing. Of all the trivial, tiny things to get on my nerves while embarking on something as major as St. Paul's conversion, Lord. Bet the Great Masters never had flies to contend with. Maybe they had other things to deal with though, like rabid dogs, mosquitos or thieves, trying to steal their work. It's the fact that it's a single fly that is really bugging me. Two's not so bad, at least there's contrast, three becomes a chord. I find there's always a lead singer, one on percussion (beating against the window) and there's always one on synth, doing any old thing.

Tuesday 31 August

Feel would like to get more involved at church, Lord. They've been calling for volunteers so now's the time to act.

My options are:

1) The sound desk. (Advantages: away from all the rabble. Disadvantages: alarming array of buttons).

2) The welcoming team. (Advantages: will be in charge of sweets and who does and doesn't get them. Disadvantages: don't think we should be giving out sweets anyway. Diabetes and obesity are rife and sugar makes kids hyper).

3) Worship flags. (Advantages: will be apt, beautiful and inspiring. Disadvantages: back could go. Also, a flag could catch on one of the candles at the front, causing a fire).

4) Cooking for the needy. (Advantages: needy will be fed. Disadvantages: a lot of work). Actually, I would really love someone to cook for me for a change.*

*PRAYER BEFORE THE LORD: Dear Lord, please prompt someone to invite me and Tim around for dinner very soon.

5) Church song editor (role have just invented). In other words, stamping out apostrophe crime and careless spellings (think this could be it Lord). I'm always spotting apostrophes in the wrong place on the screen and songs and it's got to end. What

will unbelievers think when they come to a service and see poor grammar?

2pm

Being an obedient 'w,' zipped around with the hoover, as dust-wise, things have been getting out of control (could have written my name in dust on sill in lounge). Also wrote up and printed off some posters to put up in the changing room:

'For the safety and consideration of others, please get dried in the shower area to keep the changing room floor dry. Thank you.'

What I really wanted to write was:

'Will the selfish so-and-so's who only think of their own dripping wet bodies get dried in the shower area or someone's going to go flying AND DIE!'

Tim came home for some kind of hard drive for a client and wanted to know what I was doing. Told him about my ongoing pre-pre-pre-pre-pre-pre-prep—and the posters I was going to put up. Next thing I knew was he thinks I'm wrong—that I'm acting outside the authority of the gym (meddling) and could cause trouble!

What am I meant to do Lord? I'm only trying to be an obedient 'w' and general good citizen (GGC) and yet my own husband says it's wrong!

'You're kidding?' I said, my eyes out on stalks. 'I'm saving them a job. It's because they're not stamping down on this that my accident happened in the first place. My foot really hurts now and look at the bruise on my thigh! Plus, Jane thinks it's a good idea, and she's always right'.

Stormed off in a huff.

5pm

Tim went back to work. Needing a break from having a break, I took another call about someone needing a decorator and not an artist, then I went to the gym. The Lord timed my visit perfectly—there was no one around so I could put up my posters without anyone seeing me. One poster is on the edge of the wall that separates the shower area from the changing room i.e. where it's obvious, the second is on the main changing room door—the third is on a toilet door. I will probably save someone's life by doing this. Maybe Lord You *let me slip* because You want me to sort the problem out—and You know I will. The whole thing has got *You* written all over it!

Wonder who is on cake rota at home group tonight? Think it's Liz, so should be good.

Bad thing: Have made myself a tea but can't be bothered to pick it up and drink it even though it's right next to me. Know that when I do, it'll be stone cold and then I'll have to go and put it in the microwave to re-heat it again. I'll then let it stand for a while to let the deadly gamma rays inside it subside, and forget about it all again etc etc.

10pm

Post home group report

Asked for prayer for a) work b) my foot c) St. Paul on the Road to Damascus and d) about how to volunteer at church.

Liz asked if there was something I really felt strongly about— I said the poor spelling and grammar on the screen. She said to go for it.

Tim then piped up his prayer request—for me not to put up posters in the gym. I couldn't believe it—and when have been so amazing and obedient lately, too. The room became divided. Pauline said I was being rebellious which is ridiculous as I'm the least rebellious person in the whole wide world. I'm totally obedient. Tim only has to say he wants crisps in his sandwiches and they're in there like a shot. Also, I have been composing near Michelin-starred fruits salads, adding basil to his strawberries with *balsamic vinegar*! How many husbands have wives that do that?

Tim's eyes need opening, Lord. Received prayer about it but how do you receive prayer for something you don't want prayer for? Had to stand there like a lemon and felt like a horse being led to drink, then *made* to drink. It's only posters, Lord!

Good thing: Until Tim mentioned the posters, looked like an angelic church member wanting to serve You, Lord.

Bad thing: Afterwards, looked like rebellious wife and major busy body. Told everyone that I think submission to your husband isn't about being a robot, it's about working things out together, which we simply haven't done yet. This gym thing is about me solving a social problem Lord—it's a spiritual battle in the heavenlies—not disobedience! Nor is it rising above the authority of the gym—I'm not going against them, I'm helping them! Their own piddly notice is up in tiny writing in a corner where no one goes (apart from me, obviously, but only because I went right up to it. You practically need a magnifying glass to read it).

Comforting thing: Liz's cake tonight totally amazing. A lemon roulade Delia Smith would give her back teeth for, if not her front and molars ones too. A rectangle of soft ground almond meringue with lemon curd and whipped cream, rolled into a log. Wanted to take the whole thing and shove it down my throat. When everyone was done, Liz took me to one side to pray for my foot, gently sliding in the poster situation, asking God to give me wisdom. I didn't mind, as I'm sure Jesus thinks I'm right!

Bad thing: Tim suddenly produced a box of Thornton's chocolates for general consumption. Someone gave them to us both, so shouldn't he have asked me before giving them away? It's like the three-tier Victoria sponge Lord, all over again. What's he playing at? As everyone troughed our chocs, I asked if people thought if there'd be food in heaven (as at least there won't be stealing there). We're going to be feasting nonstop, right? Stuart said he thinks there will be food in heaven but not as we know it. It will be calorie free, be special, glowing and ethereal (made by angel chefs who are there to serve us) and there will be no washing-up either. Or maybe there will be washing up but the water in heaven will be special and simply 'sparkle' the grime away. Had to stop speculating in the end, as the elderly in the group were getting tired and I was getting hungry.

In the end, I had to stand and watch the truffles disappearing with people saying how kind it was of us to bring them. Had bit of a barney about it on the way home. Tim said he was merely looking after my health (euphemism for weight again). Again he said sorry and again I forgave him. Being obedient can be a right pain.

Wednesday 1 September

8am

I love my morning coffee. I do the same thing every single morning. I grind two tablespoons of beans, put two slices of bread in the toaster, stick on the Today programme and listen to John Humphries wrestling politicians to the floor until they're squirming.

I munch my toast and look out of the window, listening to what a terrible state the world is in. Often I see a very fat wood pigeon on the garage roof. I don't think it is fat, I think it's just its bone structure. I use that excuse too.

Now that my P&M-conversion-euphoria has gone, painting has become hard again. St. Paul doesn't look like St. Paul. Have prayed and cried out for inspiration—have even prayed for the Holy Spirit to take control of my right hand and for Him to paint, not me—but since I've put brush to canvas from eight o'clock this morning, the world's most amazing apostle has gone through looking like Simon Cowell, Tim, Jeremy Corbyn and now, Peter Andre. Perhaps if I try to paint Peter Andre, I might end up with St. Paul?

Have asked Tim, who's working at home today, what he thinks of my efforts. Long silence (not good). Painted half-heartedly, then for a break, embarked on the vital and actually, very satisfying task of labelling the lids of all the herbs and spices in the cupboard.

Other things I do to avoid painting are:

This diary.

Going on Facebook and Twitter.

Sending important emails.

Taking photos of what I'm working on and labelling the images. e.g. 'Damascus1OK.jpeg', 'Damascus2terrible.jpeg' or 'Damascus3whereStPaullookslikeBruceForsyth.jpeg".

Online food shops (Morrisons, Waitrose, stuff on Amazon).

Investigating the settings on my computer for various crucial things such as Bluetooth inexplicably turning itself on which it does sometimes.

Checking that all the soap dispensers in the house are operational.

Sorting out the recycling (sometimes I need to stamp down the boxes and things in the blue bag to create more room and believe me that takes effort).

Mowing the lawn (mowing is basically a version of hoovering, although if Tim does it, it's a version of him trimming his beard)

Washing out the fridge.

Clearing out the garage (a version of washing the fridge).

Ironing (not a version of anything).

My *all-time* favourite procrastination tactic is:

Sweeping the floor and monitoring the contents of the dustpan. When we going out with one another, Tim and I had meaningful conversations. Now I go up to him with the dustpan and show him the contents.

I reckon this is what I sweep up every day:

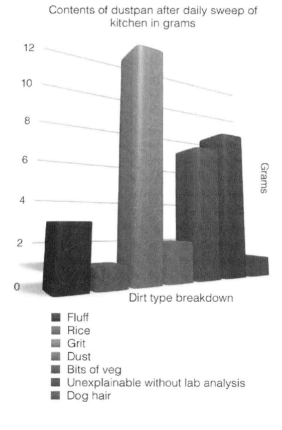

Contents of dustpan after daily sweep of kitchen in grams

Dirt type breakdown

Grams

■ Fluff
■ Rice
■ Grit
■ Dust
■ Bits of veg
■ Unexplainable without lab analysis
■ Dog hair

KAROLA WOODS

Fluff: 3g. Per year, x 365 = 1095g

Uncooked rice: 1g per day. Per year, x 365 = 365g

Grit: 12g. Per year, x 365 = 4380g

Dust: 2g. Per year, x 365 = 730g

Bits of veg: 7g. Per year, x 365 = 2555g

Unexplainable without lab analysis: 8g. Per year, x 365 = 2920g

Dog hair: 1g. Per year, x 365 = 365g

Added up that's around 8,030 grams of dirt, or 0.00803 of a metric tonne! Over ten years that would be 0.08 tonnes (leap year amount neglible suppose), and over a hundred years (which I guess would have been possible/normal in Old Testament times when people lived for ages), one whole tonne!

Behind all this cleaning is, I realise, a deep and profound dissatisfaction with my work. Caravaggio's Damascus is a masterpiece and the real St. Paul has probably got a copy of it hanging up in his room in heaven—so why am I even bothering? I mean we don't need two Romeo and Juliet's, do we? Caravaggio not only shows St. Paul going blind and stumbling to the ground, he has him falling off a dappled horse with its hoof in the air and we all know how hard horses are to draw.

Good thing: Just washed Tim's cycling gear.

Other good thing: Have started taping cocktail sticks to the side of Tim's fruit salad Tupperwares for ease of eating (O.R. 10).

Bad thing: Have terrible PMT. All I want to do is eat chocolate, cry and hide under a duvet. Am really bitter re fact Tim took those chocolates to home group the other night, Lord. I could really do with them now. I find everything becomes traumatic when I have PMT. Even carrying a mug of tea into the lounge.

I like my cup quite full too, so the slosh-&-scald potential is really quite high. At least our carpets are tea-coloured.

POSSIBLE BUSINESS IDEA BEFORE THE LORD (SHUT DOOR IF WRONG LORD, FLING OPEN IF RIGHT): A Phone App that I could design, that Tim could build, and from which we could reap huge amounts of passive income for the rest of our lives (and which we would tithe, obviously). A HOME GROUP TEA CHART THAT PEOPLE ALL OVER THE WORLD WOULD LOVE AND BUY. I have thought for a very long time now that someone should invent a tea strength app as everyone drinks tea meaning the market is huge. It would be a pie chart of a zillion different shades of brown so that if say, you were at home group, you could ask each person to pick the shade of tea that they like, add their sugar preference, and save it. I am sure people would pay 29p for this, at least. Perhaps there'd be some kind of way people could scan the cup of tea they've made and when they've got the shade right, the App bleeps or plays a little fanfare. (In another way, I can't understand why we put so much effort into getting tea right. People sometimes act as if it's the most important thing in the world).

2.30pm

Still not painting.

PMT emanating like gamma rays.

Have eaten:

A Flake

A Twirl

A packet of crisps

And had a little cry.

I know I tend to do irrational things like buy garish clothes when I have PMT, but this time Lord, I have rung and left a

message for that person back who needed a painter and
decorator for their son's room next week and said I'll do it. If
I'm not painting art, I may as well paint something, hadn't I?
Plus over the years, I've painted every room in our house Lord
and due to do the lounge soon, so… why not?

3.30pm

Finished the herb jars. Added expiry date too (nice new touch).

4pm

Still not painting. Instead, am batch-ironing. The pile of clothes
in the corner is so big, I could almost climb it, so am tackling
7-8 items at a time and feeling like Lydia the cloth-merchant
who must have ironed in some shape or form, surely. I find I
batch other activities too. I batch-paint, I batch-tidy, I batch-
sweep the floor and I batch-put-away washing-up and paper
work. Most of life is spent in one batch-activity or another,
namely moving objects around the house. The dirty clothes
come out of the washing basket in the bathroom upstairs and
into the washing machine downstairs. The saucepans come out
of the corner on the stove, are used, washed and then re-
stacked back into the corner. The rubbish ends up in the
various bins around the house, then it gets moved by me into
the big bin outside, which someone else moves somewhere
else. The shopping arrives from Waitrose/Morrisons, is then is
moved into the fridge by me, until I need to move it out again,
etc etc.

Basically, I'm not just a wife and artist Lord. I'm a household
objects movement choreographer.

Bad thing: Just made a really dud lasagne. Looked spectacular
in the tray, but when had a bit, was like eating a slab of savoury
glue. It screams 'whoever made me has really bad PMT'.
Deserves to go in the bin but can't face making anything else.
Also, would be a terrible waste of food. Why does stuff need
cooking anyway? Can't it just be put through a food processor
and whizzed around raw? Cooking is overrated Lord. Feel like

burning all my cookery books, never mind my bras. Boy is my PMT bad. Off to have a cry again.

6.30pm

Just been to the gym for a mini workout and to see if my posters are still up. They are. The main one on the wall has attracted a whole host of comments, including one person saying they'll get dried where they like and someone else saying they like my doodle of someone slipping.

How can this be rebellion, Lord? I even use locker number 30 when I come to the gym because 30 is the age when You started Your ministry. If that isn't dedication, I don't know what is!

Took ages in the shower as a) was shattered and b) wanted to see my posters in action. There are definitely more people getting dried in the correct area by the showers and Jane says she hasn't slipped once.

Will tell Tim later (and home group next week) that am clearly doing the Lord's work and this opposition is the enemy.

Got dried, tidied the changing room of litter and as no one was around, wrote a message of my own on my poster in chinagraph pencil.

SLIPPING CAN KILL

Good thing: From Find Friends, can see Tim's at B&Q, getting tester pots for the lounge. That means it will be thirty minutes until he gets home. Will time dinner for second he gets in. O.R: 100/10, surely.

Bad thing: Imogen has texted. She wants to come to stay for a week as Mark's moving out. They've split up again—this time 'for good'. Oh no Lord, I know what this means. Endless conversations about him and if splitting up is the right thing.

A clearly of-the-Lord-idea: Am going to say yes to her but will put Reg in her room so that she hears the Gospel Lord, just like P&M. Please Lord save my sister. It will hopefully make her a nicer person (just like me).

Weird thing: Reg has starting doing some new sounds. Me sweeping the floor, the printer spitting out posters and me asking in a pitiful tone, 'Have we got any chocolate in?'

That bird.

9.30pm

Off to bed soon.

Bad thing: Have only done two brush strokes today.

Other bad thing: During dinner, in PMT frenzy, burst into tears trying to extract a cornichon out of a jar. The lid wasn't the problem (for once). I just couldn't get one out of the jar as they were packed too tightly together. Tim had a go but he failed too. I then prodded at one really, really hard and prised it out but not without spattering myself all over with brine. Am going to email manufacturer and tell them what a terrible time I've had.

Good thing: In an attempt to show was not being a rebellious 'w' about the posters, got Tim a big mug of cold milk when he was on the sofa and brought him three Fox's Extremely Chocolatey biscuits. We watched a nature programme about animals dancing. I said the two greater-crested grebes running harmoniously along the water in time were me and Tim (or should be anyway). We then had a good laugh pointing at different animals and saying which of us looked like a wombat/beaver/meerkat. 1 looked like all the cute cuddly animals with big eyes and fluffy tails and Tim looked like all the assertive violent ones. Concluded we need nature, it doesn't need us.

Definite good thing which shows beyond reasonable doubt have servant heart and am not a rebellious 'w': Took charge of TV remotes as Tim hates dealing with them (as do I, actually). I know some people like to have them to stay in control—but I'm not remotely bothered about the remotes—I never have been and never will be. That said, I have no idea why so many different ones are needed in life and why there is always at least one with a mind of its own. The other thing that can happen is, often, we both get really comfy… and then we realise the remote we need is on the other side of the room. Ideally Lord, we need elasticated arms that can shoot out and retract, so that we can get things without getting up off the sofa. I would give my front teeth to someone who could invent voice-command TV. Just checked online—voice-command TV has existed for years. However, I'm not knocking my teeth out for anyone.

IDEA: Maybe we should train Reg to fetch the remotes? If he can break a brazil nut with his lethal weapon of a beak, he can bring over a remote. How would we do that though? He's probably too long in the tooth now to learn a stunt like that— he only mimics sounds. The other day when Waitrose were delivering, he started doing the phone ringing. The delivery man said I could go and answer the call if I wanted to—in the end I had to show him it was Reg and not our phone.

Very bad thing: Have run out of crisps and chocolate. Off to have another cry.

Dear Manufacturer

I am writing to complain about one of your products, a 454g jar of cornichons that I purchased recently.

I should say from the outset that there is nothing wrong with the cornichons themselves—it is the way they are packed that is the problem.

I successfully opened the jar (using a rubber glove as a grip), however I then found I could not get a single cornichon out. My husband, who is of reasonable strength and intelligence, tried and failed too.

After about five very frustrating minutes, I managed to prise one out, snapping it in the process and splattering brine all over myself (see attached photo of me in brine as proof).

Obviously it is not a huge problem next to the world's troubles, but I found it rather stressful.

Please can you give me your assurance you will consider adding one cornichon less to each jar?

I can't be the only person who has had this issue. It would also increase your profits as you'd use fewer cornichons in each jar.

I look forward to hearing from you.

Best wishes

Emily King

Thursday 2 September

6.30pm

Dear Emily

Thank you for writing to us about our 454g jar of premium pickled cornichons, priced 97 pence.

We're sorry you had trouble getting them out of the jar.

We really value what our customers think about us and we appreciate your feedback.

However, we have had no other complaints about this issue, ever, so we can only assume it's a one-off.

We suggest you buy our larger gherkins in future as they are packed slightly more loosely.

If we can be of any other assistance, please let us know.

Yours sincerely

P. Doff

Still got PMT. Got irritated with Tim this morning just as was having a pray about not getting irritated. I was in my studio on my knees when he burst in saying, 'Have you seen my thingy?!' (He didn't acknowledge I was praying or anything).

'What thingy?' I asked, trying to sound calm.

'You know, my thingy! Have you moved it?'

THE DIARY OF AN OBEDIENT WIFE

'How can I have moved it if I don't know what it is, sweetheart?' (Often add sweetheart to show am not mad when am).

He didn't answer though—he was off again, searching.

'Try your jacket pocket!" I called (good default answer).

Thirty seconds later...

'Got it!'

I still have no idea what he was talking about. He then came in again, looked at me with packed-lunch-eyes (cobbled together something) and left.

Have just printed off some litter posters to put up in the gym alongside my slipping ones. Feel like am doing the Lord's work underground.

Printed: 'For the safety and consideration of others please put your litter in the bins provided and help keep this changing room as you would like to find it'.

What I really wanted to say was, 'Stop behaving like pigs—you wouldn't throw litter around at home, would you?'

I know litter's not a huge issue, but you could skid on an empty shampoo bottle and kill yourself, couldn't you? Not to mention empty chocolate wrappers leading people (me) into temptation by reminding them that there's a vending machine outside.

Painted all afternoon—St. Paul is finally looking like St. Paul. God obviously blessing me for the act of stamping out getting dried in wrong place in the gym and taking on the litter epidemic too. Risked doing spinning at gym, the only class where I want it to end from the second it starts. It isn't too high impact on my foot, but it does make my heart feel as if it's about to explode. I pedalled so fast I thought I was going to take off into outer space. The instructor did his usual thing of yelling at us to make us go faster. He kept yelling, 'Come on

Amelia, faster! FASTER!' I kept thinking what a poor soul Amelia was and what a slowcoach she must be. Turned round to give her a quick sympathetic glance, only to see this big burly guy behind me and realised Amelia was me! Am not going back to that class in a hurry.

Afterwards, had a monitor of my posters, then got into the jacuzzi. Jane was there. Told her about my posters. Jane very surprised re Tim's/home group's attitude but I could see she had 'you need to be obedient to Tim, Emily' written all over her face and she looked a bit awkward at having encouraged me.

We changed subject after that and compared the nail varnish on our toes. Hers—which I can say hand on heart has been on those toes of hers for at least two weeks, is still immaculate—whereas my (new) nail varnish is chipping, big time. Apparently, I've been putting on nail varnish wrong all my life, just like I'd been making tea wrong all my life *Base and top coats are vital.* You're meant to do base coat, colour coat, top coat, like a nail varnish sandwich. It seems so obvious now but I've only ever had time to one coat Lord. That must be why hers stays on so well and mine looks shocking. I might have a bottle of undercoat somewhere—but given I've found it hard enough to doing one coat, how am I ever going to have time to do three? Jane says because she does it properly once, it saves her hours in the long run (good point) and that she does her nails before her morning prayers so they have time to dry (another good point).

We stayed in jacuzzi for at least fifteen minutes and I felt like a vegetable cooking in a pan. I couldn't face getting out even though the ends of my fingers and toes were wrinkling like walnuts. I was one millimetre away from offering to pay someone £10 to carry me out of the jacuzzi, then shower, dry and dress me and then take me home and put me to bed like a baby. The only thing that got me out in the end was the thought of having dinner at home (M&S curries).

Gemma rang to see if I would mind making a cake for her and Kieran's wedding in a couple of weeks' time. Not the actual wedding cake itself (relief) just one of the many cakes they're putting out after the service.

CULINARY WORD OF KNOWLEDGE: Feel led to make Gemma and Kieran a croquembouche—a vastly complex cone of profiteroles which are stuck together with molten sugar and have a crazy nest of spun sugar on top. Will probably have a nervous breakdown (NBD) making it, but it'll be worth it.

Bad thing: Have realised am harbouring bitterness towards Gemma for never returning a rather rare, unlabelled pudding-bowl-shaped Tupperware that she once borrowed to make a steamed lemon sponge in. I asked for it back once (really politely) but it got me nowhere. So now, not only has she got my rare bowl Lord, I've also got to go and make her a cake for her wedding, practically rewarding her for not returning my possessions. I can't believe the whole Tupperware thing runs so deep Lord! I clearly haven't forgiven her yet.

Tricky thing: Tim has just applied eight tester pots to a corner of the lounge. I like one called Crispy Crumble, as it's the exact colour of apple crumble (the topping bit anyway). He likes a pale green one (the colour of cornichons and really awful).

Dear Lord, please help me to be: 'Slow to speak, quick to anger and slow to listen.' Oops. I do of course mean: 'Slow to speak, *slow* to anger and *quick* to listen'.

Friday 3 September

9am

Things Tim does that bug me, big time:

1) He leaves his Crocs in the middle of the room so that I always go flying over them, nearly killing myself in the process. The only way around this, I've realised, is to wear his Crocs myself. He then starts to look for them and finally discovers

I've got them on my feet, which he doesn't like. SOLUTION: PRAY, NOT PUT HIS CROCS ON, BUT LOOK WHERE I AM GOING. IF I FORGET TO AND GO FLYING, I MUST SEE IT AS AN OPPORTUNITY FOR QUICKENING MY REFLEXES. ACTUALLY, THEY'RE ALREADY PRETTY QUICK. ONCE WHEN I FELL OVER HIS CROCS, I SKIDDED ACROSS THE FLOOR, NEARLY CRACKING MY SKULL OPEN ON THE GRANITE WORK TOP—BUT MY SUPER QUICK REFLEXES MEANT I REGAINED MY BALANCE JUST IN TIME BY GRABBING ONTO THE SIDE OF A CHAIR. THOUGHT IT WAS CURTAINS.

2) He puts things back in the garage the wrong way i.e. he leaves everything at the front rather than putting things to the back or down the side. When I open the garage and need something from the back there are about ten things I have to climb over before I can get to what I need. I have asked him not to do this Lord, but he still does. SOLUTION: PRAY, BUT ALSO SEE THE MOVING/CLIMBING OVER THINGS AS AN OPPORTUNITY FOR FUN/EXERCISE. OR, HAVE SECOND ENTRANCE MADE AT BACK SO CAN GET IN THAT WAY.

3) On holiday, when we're utterly and hopelessly lost, instead of getting out a map, Tim starts to walk in any direction like a clockwork toy. SOLUTION: PRAY, BUT ALSO REEL HIM IN LIKE A FISH, GENTLY BUT FIRMLY SAYING, 'THIS WAY TIM.' THEN CALL 999/HELICOPTER RESCUE OR START TO BUILD A SMALL FIRE WITH WHICH TO MAKE SMOKE SIGNALS.

4) Leaving used tissues everywhere. SOLUTION: PRAY, BUT ALSO, COUNT TO TEN BEFORE LOSING IT AND ASK HIM NICELY NOT TO DO THAT. FAILING THAT, JUST TIDY THEM AWAY.

5) He comments on my driving. If he's tired it's worse. I get 'WATCH OUT!' as if I'm about to drive head first into a bus

or something. I'm a confident driver when I'm on my own, in pieces when he's there. SOLUTION: PRAY, BUT ALSO, DRIVE AT 5 MPH, SAY SORRY ALL THE TIME, AND DO EVERYTHING HE SAYS (EVEN THOUGH I'M DOING IT ALREADY).

6) I don't know how he does it, but Tim always gets to sofa in the evening before I get to my comfy chair. Yes he may have done the dishes and stacked the dishwasher and he may have even made our hot drinks, but he's still on that sofa while I'm doing things like sweeping the floor or updating the fridge and freezer chart contents. SOLUTION: PRAY, BUT ALSO, PLONK MYSELF ON ARMCHAIR STRAIGHT AFTER DINNER AND LEAVE JOBS UNTIL TOMORROW INSTEAD OF RUNNING AROUND LIKE A HEADLESS CHICKEN.

7) Forgetting his packed lunch. SOLUTION: PRAY, BUT ALSO, SET UP A TRIP SYSTEM SO THAT WHEN HE LEAVES THE HOUSE WITHOUT IT, AN ALARM AND FLASHING LIGHTS GO OFF AND A BANNER UNFURLS ACROSS THE CAR DOOR SAYING 'HAVE YOU GOT YOUR PACKED LUNCH, HON?'

8) When I'm cooking, Tim always, always looks at the hob as if something on it is about to explode or catch fire. I CANNOT THINK OF A SOLUTION FOR THIS OTHER THAN TO YELL 'STOP LOOKING AT THE HOB!'

9) When he's serving up dinner he always says, 'How much do you want?' To which I always answer, 'An average portion'. I can't understand why he does this Lord! When you go to a restaurant, they don't ask, 'How much do you want?' SOLUTION: PRAY, BUT ALSO STATE AT OUTSET HOW MANY PORTIONS MEAL IS INTENDED FOR E.G. 2, OR 4… so he can divide it in his head there and then. (I know what's confused things Lord—it's a phase I had of serving up just a little so we could then have seconds. IT

WOULD HAVE BEEN BETTER NOT TO HAVE DONE THAT AS IT'S MUDDIED THE WATERS).

10) Feel there should be a number ten but can't think of anything just yet. Oh I know. Tim is always. always on his phone yet the minute I try to get him on it, there's never any answer. SOLUTION: PRAY, BUT ALSO KEEP TRYING SO THAT AT LEAST WHEN HE DOES GET TO IT HE SEES THERE'S BEEN 39 MISSED CALLS. Alternatively, try the landline.

Noon

Been wondering if am a dedicated helper wife who upholds and encourages her husband in everything he does (apart from the 10 earlier moans) and have decided that I am. Today, in the pouring rain, went into town to the cobblers to buy Tim some laces for his new shoes (one of them broke the second he put them on). The shop, which also does keys (have never quite got the link between keys and shoes Lord and why they're always dealt with in the same place) had all kinds of laces too. Long ones, short ones, flat ones, round ones, round polished ones, sporty ones, 100cm ones, 70cm ones. Thought, who on earth buys 100cm laces, Lord? Someone with thigh length boots? Or a clown with long shoes? I haven't seen a clown with long shoes on for years, let alone one needing laces. Not only did I go there in the pouring rain when I had loads of work to do, I also enquired if they had a way of fixing squeaky shoes as Tim has a pair that do that (sadly, forgot to bring them with me). Said I'd tried getting rid of the squeak myself by removing the insole (didn't work), soaking the sole (didn't work) putting a tissue underneath the sole (still didn't work), and then I read online that you can somehow fill in the crack with some kind of builder's caulk substance (beyond my capabilities). I even *lay on the floor* with my head on the carpet on day, as Tim walked up and down the room in them to ascertain where in the shoe the squeak was coming from. Asked Tim how many women in the country have done *that* for their husbands—he said probably none. The cobbler said there is nothing we can do, just live with the squeak.

QUESTION BEFORE THE LORD: Is trying to be a really great wife getting in the way of me doing my work? What is being a great wife anyway?

1pm

Just taken a page out of Jane's book and have done my nails 'sandwich-style'. This is so I can be beautiful not just on the inside but on the outside too. Have to say, sandwich-style varnish is a major faff. Half way through I thought, I never show my toe nails to anyone anyway, so what is the point? The only people who see my toenails are me, Tim, Reg (who is a bird), Pluto (who is a dog) and the people in the changing room who never look at my toenails anyway. Really, apart from Tim, I'm the only person who sees my toes and to be honest, I don't spend that much time looking at them either (who in their right mind would?) Anyway, just like Jane, I've done them before my readings and prayers, so that they dry before I go to the gym.

3pm

Jane must pray for much longer than me, as when I got to the gym at 1.30, when I took my socks off, they'd stuck to my toenails, Lord. I had to tear them away, leaving sock fluff on my nails and varnish on my socks.

At least have had a reasonable day on Damascus but it's going very slowly. (This painting is going to have a longer gestation period than an elephant).

7pm

Washed out the fridge after dinner. In the bottom left drawer, found a lump of something furry that I think was ginger originally but now looked like a slug.

Bad thing: Tim disagreeing with me when I said my PMT craving for chocolate was medicinal (was ransacking the house for a 3-pack of Flakes at the time). He then asked me if am taking my Evening Primrose Oil regularly and if the dose is strong enough. Burst into tears.

Gracious thing: While sobbing, didn't answer back. Said, 'I'm not going to say anything! I just need to be horizontal and lie in a darkened room!' Sometimes I think I have PMT all the time and it's not PMT, it's just 'T'.

Final bad thing: Although I couldn't find Flakes I did find a mini Milky Way. Nearly had a (NBD) nervous breakdown opening it though. Tried tearing the perforated edge (failed), then tried biting it (failed). In end, had to rifle through drawers to find a pair of scissors with which to stab it open (felt as if was killing it).

Saturday 4 September

Been caught out by own posters, Lord. While Tim went to B&Q to get more tester pots, I thought I'd leave him to it and have a swim. Was loitering in shower afterwards, monitoring where people were getting dried and if they were leaving litter, when I heard my phone ring in my locker. It was Tim's ringtone, (which he's made Matt Redman's '10, 000 Reasons').

Knowing he only rings from B&Q when it's an absolute emergency, hared over to the locker, dripping wet. Lo and behold, a woman in a red swimming costume shot out from around the corner and said, 'Excuse me love, have you seen the posters? About getting dried near the showers—and not getting the floor wet for other people? You're going to cause an accident!'

'You're right,' I said, standing there shocked, dripping and naked, with 'Sing like never before, oh my soul' playing in the background. 'It's just that...'

'Excuses, excuses,' red costume woman (RCW) said. 'Everyone does what they like, that's the problem'.

'I agree,' I said. 'I totally agree. The posters are *mine!*' I blurted out. (Felt glow of victory as her confusion grew). 'I put them up as I was fed up of slipping and people getting dried all over the place. I only dashed over because my husband's in B&Q and when he rings from there I know it's a matter of life or death. Shows they're working though, as you took note of them!'

Matt Redman long gone, I started to take the posters down.

Just then, a woman from reception came in and saw me.

'Er, excuse me, I was just about to do that'.

'So, they aren't your posters then?' said RCW to the receptionist, flashing me a glance.

'No. Someone's put them up and caused a right furore'.

'But the floor is *dryer*,' said RCW to the receptionist. 'So you do need them. You've only got a small sign over there'. (Suddenly, me and RCW were allies).

'I know, but people can't just go sticking up posters whenever they like, can they? I mean we've got litter posters too now. What next, shower before you swim?'

Yes yes yes! Absolutely! Hardly anyone showers before they swim anymore and they should! The receptionist went and RCW disappeared back into her cubicle.

Rang Tim back when I got into the car. All he wanted to know was if we needed a dust-sheet for when I do the lounge. I said we had one but he's bought one anyway, meaning we'll have to go back to B&Q to return it.

Then went to have my haircut. Bit of an impulse thing—just marched into a random salon and they slotted me in (they had hardly any appointments booked in, now I know why). Basically they've given me a Hitler haircut, Lord. It's sort of short yet floppy and it being dark definitely doesn't help. Where oh where is the justice in that, Lord? The weird thing is, someone before me had a haircut done that made them look just like Richard III, so I think this hairdresser specialises in despot haircuts.

QUESTION BEFORE THE LORD: Why are women's haircuts more expensive than men's? I can understand when long hair is involved, but when it's short, they should cost the same. Next time I need my hair cutting, I'm going to go into a barber's and say feel like, 'Hello, I have short hair and I need a bit of a trim. Can you just pretend that I'm a man? I can wear a false beard, if it helps'.

When I got home, I casually asked Tim if I looked like Hitler (casual is best to elicit honest reaction). He said no about a thousand times but I do not believe him.

Have tidied spare room for Imogen who's arriving later. (She'll tell me if I look like 'H' or not).

In other news, have got my painting and decorating gear ready for next week—long white overalls, masking tape, brushes. 'You're organized,' said Tim (he thinks it's for when I do our lounge).

Bad thing: The new tester pots he got are no good either, so when we return the dust sheet, we need to get some more.

Is there no end to DIY Lord? I don't like Tim cycling around all these big roundabouts.

10.45pm

Went to a small Thai restaurant with Jane and some friends from church to celebrate her birthday. I gave her a small still life water colour I did ages ago of some flowers. She really loved it—as did everyone else—but neither she nor anyone else there said anything about my hair. *If no-one in your loving church family can say anything positive about your new hair cut Lord, it must be bad.*

Had chicken satay skewers for starter, followed by some kind of squid which came in tubes with diagonal patterns cut into it. Had to wait for ages as it was busy.

It made me think of the parable of the five thousand that I read this morning. One of the things I noticed is how quickly the whole thing happened, with no delays or anything. They were hungry one minute, fed the next. And how smoothly and easily it all seemed to go. No talk of who gave the food out, or if orderly queues were formed, or if they were served group by group or buffet style. And, most importantly, who cleared up? There must have been an inordinate amount of fish skin/bones left over and it would have been really messy to eat as well. Maybe seagulls ate all the debris, Lord?

If Jesus did this miracle now, it would need to be cod/haddock and chips with a curry sauce/pea option and they'd need to be in those white foam boxes with sachets of salt and vinegar. Basically, I'd really like to know the details of this miracle Lord, as I find cooking and clearing up after home group (tossing around eight mugs and plates into the dishwasher) really stressful.

Wore a dark top to the restaurant as am trying to overcome the stronghold of splodging my clothes in public places and am desperately trying to be more sophisticated too. Jane wore pale lemon and didn't get *anything* down her pale green top and she wasn't even trying. Told her about RCW and the posters. She hasn't met anyone she likes on her dating site yet but she had glittery nail varnish on which looked amazing. Have asked her to text me when she does them next and I'll do mine at the same time and in the same way so there can be no failure.

Good thing: The restaurant had one of those red and gold ceramic good luck cats with a waving arm by the till. Prayed for it to explode and show the owners the error of their ways.

Bad thing: As drove home, got a bit lost. Am sure I made a three mile journey nine (didn't tell Tim as it was a clear waste of petrol).

Beautiful thing: As drove through the night, saw a barn owl flash past with a big white face.

Other good thing: Had nice moment with Tim. He wanted the iPad but I was on the sofa and he was on the armchair opposite. I stretched out to pass it to him and it felt like that moment in the Sistine Chapel where God reaches out his hand and touches Adam. Looked at Tim fondly and thought, he is wonderful, even if he never squeezes out the washing-up sponge properly so that billions of bacteria breed on it every second.

Tim noticed a small splodge down my top. Splodging stronghold still clearly here.

Sunday 5 September

Imogen arrived late last night. She had to park on the blind corner because WGM is here. The first thing she said was, 'Emily, what'd happened to your hair? You look like Hitler!'

I'm going to have a wear a hat permanently now Lord. How do I go out—do anything—if I look like one of the world's worst tyrants? Even sandwich-style nail varnish won't change that.

Went to church this morning with a hair clip in my fringe in an attempt to look more normal. Imogen didn't come.

Before the service started, I volunteered to do the computer. Tony-who-does-everything-at-church-including-co-ordinating-volunteers almost hyperventilated, saying I was an 'answer to prayer'. Need to go in for training at some point this week—haven't said primary motive is eradicating poor spelling and grammar.

Angela had a word of knowledge about someone having a pain in their neck and God wanting to heal it. At first, thought perhaps it was metaphorical and that Pauline should go forward. Interestingly, I then realised that *I'd* just got a major crick in my neck through trying to see the label on Alison the senior leader's wife's new dress as I wanted to know where she'd got it from—she always wears nice clothes that are understated and look as if they've been thrown together. Just as I was beginning to think the word of knowledge might be for me, a man with a surgical collar around his neck came forward. *What took him so long Lord?* Now I know how You must have felt Lord with the man by the pool!

Tim and I then popped to B&Q to take the dust sheet back and get more tester pots. I also got a massive tub of white for this child's room I'm doing—Imogen's agreed to help. (Tim thinks I'm mad but I think it's all grist to the mill).

If there is one thing I never expected when I said 'I do' Lord, it's the amount of times we've been to B&Q. We're there *all the time*. During a recent spate of visits when we were trying to buy a lampshade, I was there so often, I got on first name terms with the woman in the lighting and invited her to Alpha.

Whenever we need to go now, it's usually to choose paint, pick up mixed paint we've ordered (love that crazy paint-mixing machine that jigs around) or exchange something because it was an impulse buy and we should never have bought it in the first place. Or, like in this case, because we've a duplicate (the dust sheet).

Saw Guy from church who a) initially looked guilty for having been seen *by us* in B&Q on a Sunday b) then immediately looked surprised for seeing *us* in B&Q on a Sunday. He said he wasn't sure if it was right to shop in B&Q on a Sunday (or anywhere else for that matter) but seeing us there alleviated him from his guilt.

Thought of pointing out we weren't actually shopping, we were getting a refund (i.e. shopping in reverse), but didn't because of the extra tester pots we'd found. Said it wasn't a crime to shop on a Sunday and that it's the spirit with which it's done that counts, and that it should be done with the context of rest from one's own job (said he works in painting and decorating).

Came home, threw together a ploughman's lunch and tried out the latest round of colours on a section of the lounge. While Imogen went out to call Mark to check if it is over (it is) and while we waited for the tester paints to dry, Tim and I shared a time of prayer and worship together (we often do this when faced with important decisions such as what colour to paint the lounge). Tim found The Splendour of a King on You Tube. We hit play, knelt, then waited for the ad to play its few compulsory seconds before we hit skip. There was a really long instrumental section that went on and on and on and on. It didn't just go on for like, twenty seconds, it went on *for ages*. We both knelt there, heads bowed, waiting and waiting. When it still hadn't started after about five minutes, and this woman started speaking out totally unrelated scriptures and prayers in a shimmery kind of way, we looked up at one in despair. Just start will you, *start*!

Eventually Tim said, 'It isn't the right version, Em'. Neither of us had any desire to worship or pray after that, we just wanted to chop the TV to bits.

Bad thing: Imogen walked into the lounge in the middle of it all.

Other bad thing: We still can't agree on any of the colour of the lounge. Suggested mixing them all together as a compromise, or painting the lounge in different coloured stripes, or choosing a colour neither of us likes so that we're both unhappy.

Yet another bad thing: Imogen has brought packets of this vegetarian protein called seitan (pronounced Satan) into the house. (She's just made herself a Satan sandwich, Lord).

Strange thing: Just found a tiny spring about 3mm in diameter and about 15mm long in our bowl on the kitchen table full of important knick-knacks i.e. junk. Where did it come from and is it important? Because neither me nor Tim will ever find out, it will never get thrown out, in case one day, we find out it's crucial for something. Has it sprung out of the microwave or just come out of a pen? As Tim isn't around to ask, have put it back in the bowl for another day...

Good thing: Sewed buttons onto Tim's jacket as the threads were coming loose (is nothing made properly anymore Lord?) Did it in front of Tim and Imogen to look like a 100% devoted wife but....

Bad thing: Got so stressed stabbing self with needle and getting blood everywhere that told Tim that next time he had a loose button, he could sew it on himself, thereby defeating whole object of being a good witness for my lost sister.

5pm

Dinner with Karen and James tonight. Imogen having a night in staring at her phone, texting Mark who is leaving their flat as I write. They don't see eye to eye on anything, have different values and interests and want different things, yet she still thinks it can work.

Have hidden my new nail varnish set, the special Clarins bath gel that Tim got me (so special that even I don't use it) and all my chocolate in my sister-proof undies drawer as I know what Imogen is like.

Dear Chief Executive of B&Q

I am writing to you as one of your most loyal and regular customers.

My husband and I have been to your store many times over the past few years, spending hundreds if not thousands of pounds.

The reasons I'm writing is that we're coming to the store quite a lot at the moment because we're trying to find a colour for our lounge and I'm worried that seeing your logo so often will make it permanently emblazoned on my retinas. I'm also concerned that I won't be able to get the electronic voice promising assistance out of my head (it automatically comes on when the self-service till goes wrong).

Please could you open some small, modest hotels in the vicinity of your stores? This would give your customers some time to think instead of going all the way back home and realising they need to return, often the same day.

Perhaps the rooms could be small, orange, modern B&Q pods where one weary spouse can have a rest in the dark for a few hours—while the other one continues to roam through the store, looking for the right aisle and being distracted by all the special offers you have on (it's always the special offers that get you. Ice-scrapers for windscreens, rolls of sellotape, bumper packs of those micro cloths. Personally, I have a soft spot for those bottles of Baby Bio).

The rooms don't need to be luxurious, although a mini-bar with a few bags of complimentary roasted peanuts wouldn't go amiss.

Finally, perhaps there could also be a marriage counselling section in the corner of your stores, to help couples resolve interior design disputes? My husband and I are starting to have a few ding-dongs about what colour paint to go for—and someone independent to talk to would really help. Perhaps alongside someone doing colour blindness tests, too?

Best wishes and many thanks

Mrs Emily King

Monday 6 September

8.50am

If there's a prayer I think God sometimes rolls his eyes at it's, 'Help me, Lord. Help me help me help me, help me help me help me'. Sometimes, I say it all day long. Am sure God often just wants to say, 'Obey my Word Emily, and that'll help you quite a lot'.

Imogen having Satan on toast for breakfast. She would have been going on holiday to Greece with Mark this week.

Last night's meal at Karen and James's left a lot to be desired. I mean it's not as if I don't go to a huge amount of effort when someone comes round to ours, is it? I'm only expecting to be treated as I treat others, and that's Biblical, isn't it? I've been known to plan menus months in advance and rehearse new recipes. When I prayed to be invited to dinner Lord, I should have also prayed for someone who can cook.

All we had was:

Pizza (shop-bought), garlic bread (shop-bought) and ice-cream with chocolate biscuits (shop-bought). No vegetables anywhere. Felt myself getting scurvy by the minute. Homemade pesto on pasta would have been better. Homemade anything. I may have been smiling on the outside, but on the inside, I was crying. Am therefore thinking of compiling a questionnaire for people to fill out before I go round to their home.

Possible things to ask:

1) What is your favourite meal?

2) What is your favourite pudding?

3) Do you watch Masterchef?

4) Do you watch Bake Off?

5) Would you class yourself as a B.O./M.C. contestant who has i) a realistic chance of winning ii) a slight chance of winning iii) no chance at all, you only want to be on TV?

6) What is the difference between a Swiss meringue, an Italian meringue and a French meringue?

7) How would you make and maintain a sourdough starter?

8) If something says bake at 170C—what is this as a) fan b) gas? c) Fahrenheit?

9) What is a bain-marie?

10) What is the dish you are most likely to make at a dinner party?

When we came home I took a vitamin tablet.

Bad thing: Imogen was freaked out by Reg doing sound of creaking boards while we were out. He only ever did them when she was out of the room so she thought that someone else was in the house with her.

Other bad thing: She also said Reg swore and told himself off all evening. Explained the swearing is the previous owner, the telling off is me and Tim. So much for Reg preaching the gospel.

Yet another bad thing: Tim has forgotten his packed lunch (raw milk gruyere on sourdough). I went to so much effort Lord, wrapping it in greaseproof paper and everything.

Final bad thing: Spiked up my hair this morning to try to look less Hitlerish. Tim said looked as if had put a finger in a socket.

6pm

Imogen came into the lounge in some lovely open slippers. She only had my new nail varnish on. *She'd gone rifling through my knicker drawer Lord, when we were out.*

'My underwear drawer is private!' I yelled in a slightly unhinged way.

She only wanted a bit of chocolate she said, and tried all the sister-proof places she knows I use until she found it. She then also found my bath gel, used half of it in the bath (along with all the hot water), then she did her nails with my nail varnish and ate the chocolate while watching TV. (Sounds like she had a nice evening Lord, much nicer than ours).

All my life she's nicked off with my things and yet again I feel as if I've been a total doormat (bathmat to be more precise). To cap it all, she's spilled red wine on the carpet in her room and poured my £5 a tub, hand-raked, Fleur de Sel de Camargue sea salt on it to try to get rid of it.

a) What is she doing with wine in her room?

and

b) Why didn't she use Saxa?

She also said I need a new bra as the flesh-coloured one she 'fleetingly saw' was like a pair of old Cornish Pasties.

Went off in a huff and watched various videos on YouTube on how to make Gemma's wedding croquembouche.

Bad thing: Reg incessantly repeating 'my underwear drawer is private' in slightly crazy way.

Other bad thing: Imogen says the light is wrong in my painting Lord. Maddeningly, she's right.

Tuesday 7 September

Today, as was getting up, was about to moan about something... can't remember what, but it started off, 'My life... my life…' Tim interrupted me saying, 'Is much better with your husband in it?' 'Yes,' I said, snapping out of it quickly. I picked up the tights I had on yesterday—they bulged out at the knees. Showed them to Tim and they made him laugh.

Painted St Paul this morning, asking God to infuse my painting like Waitrose garlic-infused olive oil. Imogen quite helpful really (she could have been an artist too Lord) and have made great strides.

We went for a coffee and she told me all about Mark. I must become a better listener Lord. I can't help but glaze over when she ~~goes on about~~ talks about him.

Ways can listen to Imogen more effectively:

Never ever take eyes off her. Nod lots. Repeat back what she says, even if my eyes are glassy and I sound robotic. Say 'Uh-huh, how terrible'. Practise expressions of concern and compassion.

Went to French Connection—or Imogen did anyway. While she browsed for clothes/shoes/jewellery because of the deep spiritual void in her life, I popped to Lakeland (my favourite shop of all time) for a croquembouche mould for Gemma's cake next month (need to start practising *now*). Have to say am really looking forward to making this croquembouche. It's going to be my most ambitious culinary attempt ever. The videos on YouTube vary from high class French patisserie chefs to an Australian bloke stacking around a hundred profiteroles around a traffic cone.

The very helpful assistant said they used to do the moulds but sadly, they've been discontinued. Instead, I bought some new rubber gloves that am totally in love with (got three for the price of two). They're off-white, moisturising, anti-bacterial with interior white flocking and I can honestly say I feel victorious in them.*

*THOUGHT: Perhaps Lord, I could wear them as ordinary gloves too, when out walking Pluto? Discretely, of course, so that I don't look mad. My ordinary ones just don't cut it in bad weather. To be honest, Lord, I don't know why You didn't create us (women) with rubber-coated hands in the first place, with all the cooking and cleaning we do. Rubber or silicon feet would have been good too, as then we wouldn't need loads of pairs of shoes either (although I love shoes). The mountain of rubbish each person must create and send to landfill during their lifetime... If someone were to take a very deep sample of the earth and pull it out, like a cheese-maker does with a round of cheese, they'd be able to analyse all the strata of rubbish and see how household items have changed over the years. The findings could then go into a special Museum of Rubbish.

Went to Hobbycraft next, that amazing shop that actually, after Lakeland, M&S, TK Maxx, Aldi, Lidl and B&Q, sells everything you need in life plus much more. They didn't have croquembouche tins either. Thought would buy a sheet of A1 card and make a cone myself but then found an amazing 12-inch high polystyrene cone which will be perfect. Not sure what people use these cones for normally, as they weren't in bakeware but in crafts. Floral arrangements? Bases for a pointy hat? The things people do.

To finish off, we went to the gym for a nice relaxing swim. The receptionist was amazed to hear Imogen was my sister. 'You don't look at all alike,' she said (Imogen looking particularly slim and beautiful at the time).

Annoying thing: If Imogen looks miserable, she still looks beautiful in a sulky-model-kind of a way. With me, even when I'm on top of the world, strangers come up to me and go, 'Cheer up, it hasn't happened yet'. I find I have to wear a smile just to shut people up Lord, but I thought Christians were meant to be full of joy and shine all the time?

To my horror I saw that Imogen has 'Mark' tattooed on her shoulder. Asked her what is she going to do now they're not together anymore—only have boyfriends called Mark? We swam and talked side by side (hate it when people do that but we did it anyway).

Two minutes later, crucifix serpent bloke came in and started chatting up Imogen.

Typical of her to:

a) attract a weirdo and

b) not find them weird and

c) get male attention wherever she goes (I've swum in this pool for months without my wedding ring on and NO ONE—not even someone over 80—has looked at me once).

Swam off in a huff doing backstroke to drown out their voices.

Bad thing: Nearly cracked my head open on the side as forgot edge was coming up.

Good thing: As swam, comforted myself with knowledge that am a child of God and unconditionally loved. Also by thinking about how much I'm going to enjoy the stash of chocolate Imogen's bought me to replace what she stole.

Other bad thing: Crucifix/serpent (Mick) and Imogen have swapped numbers. When will she learn? She's not even over Mark yet Lord.

Other good thing: While waiting for Imogen to dry her hair, practised expressions of compassion and concern in the changing-room mirror. Am bound to need them at some point very soon.

5pm

Home group tonight. Felt led to invite Imogen and praise the Lord, she is coming. God has heard my cries.

Theme is going to be generosity and us all praying to be more generous. To be honest Lord, I think I'm too generous and I want to ask the group to pray for me to have the wisdom to know when I should be *less* generous. I'm always doing something for someone and frankly, it can be a right pain. Imogen says she's into meditation at the moment as it helps clear her mind. I said Christians meditate too, but we focus on Jesus and His Word, asking the God of the whole Universe who loves us to intervene and help. She then replied she doesn't want a crutch, she wants to sort stuff out by herself (exactly, that's the problem).

AREA OF GROWTH: Letting Imogen have last word on meditation. Am becoming so mature, it's untrue.

OTHER AREA OF GROWTH: My hips. Have put on two pounds. Crazy how half the world has too much, the other half, too little.

YET ANOTHER AREA OF GROWTH: Have given a pair of my new rubber gloves to Imogen to show that I can be generous when I want to be.

URGENT PRAYER: Dear Lord. Please may our group tonight focus more on You rather than on 'local news' (gossip) or on who has or hasn't brought what kind of cake—so that Imogen might come to know You Lord and be saved.

Bad thing: Imogen has been teaching Reg new swear words and 'Emily is a ninny'. Explained the power of proclamation to her, and the curse that she is basically getting my own pet to speak out over me in the heavenly realms. That shut her up.

11.30pm

Just back from home group. Imogen said it was nice. Nice? How about powerful, anointed or holy? We aren't going to save the lost by being nice Lord, are we? Must trust a seed's been planted. Although Imogen must have had fields of seeds planted in her by now. Liz did tell her it wasn't about rules—but about faith in Jesus, a personal relationship with God and a whole new life. Imogen said she does believe in Jesus (but He isn't Lord of her life. She's doing her own thing).

Had prayer for my painting of St. Paul on the Road to Damascus which at the moment is well and truly driving me around the bend. Stuart said if art were easy then everyone would be doing it (they are though). Then Liz said anything worth doing needs to be fought over in prayer.

Then, Tim raised the issue of the colour of our lounge as a prayer request. I couldn't believe it Lord, not after the saga of the posters! Are we meant to have no privacy Lord? Tim said it's not so much the colour he's bothered about, it's how we go about choosing it. 'You just want green,' wanted to say, but didn't. Received prayer about putting one another before ourselves, which logically means I have to agree to green and Tim has to agree to Crispy Crumble. Asked him why he keeps bringing up really personal things at home group. He said the more personal and honest we are at group, the more it encourages others to be the same (annoying but true).

During the discussion on generosity, when Stuart asked us to identify a time when we could have been more generous, Imogen stared at me, wiggling her painted toenails. 'What about the rubber gloves?' I mouthed. Stuart said we can never out give God and that whatever hardship we're going through where we think God might have forgotten us, we need to remember God gave His son and that will give us perspective. Imogen then told the group that her main objection to becoming a Christian is that she doesn't think Christians have any fun.

'That's ridiculous!' I said. 'I'm always having fun'. 'When?' Imogen asked. 'I have fun some of the time,' I replied. 'OK then, hardly ever—but I nearly do, now and again!'

I get what she means though; people do have fears like that. Before I became a Christian, the things I feared most were:

a) Thinking that I'd end up wearing really horrid sandals.

b) That I'd start putting up posters of rainbows and flowers everywhere with Bible verses on them.

c) And that I'd stop shaving my legs.

Actually, all these things have happened.

Pauline wasn't on the cake rota but had brought some very artificial-looking mini Chocolate Swiss Rolls for us all. Ate one graciously (overly light and sugary). Then put another whole one in my mouth horizontally and took a swig of tea so that an ecstatic sweet hot chocolate soup formed in my mouth. Made

Imogen laugh (thereby proving Christians can at least be funny).

<u>Home group bombshell</u>: Stuart and Liz want to trial a new 'biscuits only' regime to relieve people of the burden of baking (Pauline will obviously not feel the benefit). Am quite sad as really like baking and didn't see it as a burden at all, or a nice one at least.

Major announcement that must be of the Lord as it's not something I want in any way, shape or form: To prove am a 100% obedient wife, have decided to submit to Tim and agree to the green even though it's awful. (O.R. a million).

Tim bit baffled and says he's quite happy to have the Crispy Crumble after all and that I'm probably right—it does go better with all our furnishings (knew it).

'No no Tim,' I said. 'If it's green you want, green it shall be'. Can't believe he's changing his mind at this stage Lord. Better to submit to him for something I don't want, than something I do, surely. (It isn't submission otherwise, is it?)

Was still bit peckish when came home after group. Whenever I want a snack Tim always says, 'Have some air. It's calorie free, fat free, gluten free, air-miles free, needs no cooking and you won't feel guilty afterwards'. I'm surprised I'm not a skeleton Lord.

'We're getting the green,' were my final words, as we switched off the light.

Wednesday 8 September

Went painting with Imogen all day—a guy's house who's just moved somewhere on his own and wants his son's rooms doing for when he comes round (he's newly separated).

HIS NAME IS MARK LORD AND I THINK HE LIKES IMOGEN.

Managed to spatter face with emulsion while doing ceiling (should have brought goggles).

Jumped in shower when got back and scrubbed my face with a scourer. How many women in the world can say they've done that? None, probably. Imogen used proper facial scrub from the Body Shop with bits of ground nut shell in it. Her face glowed afterwards (but so did mine).

She and Mark have exchanged numbers, just like she did with crucifix serpent man in the pool. I said she was mad, they'll both be on the rebound, not just her. (At least she won't have to shell out for a new tattoo with him though).

Tim pleased our emulsion-ing went well—quality time spent with Imogen etc and which didn't involve shopping for clothes. Personally, I never want to decorate someone else's house ever again. Too much pressure and too much like hard work.

Thursday 9 September

8.30am

Started painting very early this morning. In spite of yesterday's back-breaking work, I think it's moved something in the heavenlies. St. Paul is coming along very nicely (thank You Lord).

I had to switch on my computer just now because Tim keeps switching it off last thing at night. I then have to reboot it every morning and it takes ages. He of all people must know a reboot takes up more power than when it's on sleep!

He has also forgotten his packed lunch yet again. I put a Post-It note on the fridge, on the kettle, the back door and on his handlebars but he still forgot it. How can he miss four Post-Its, Lord?

Imogen's still in bed.

11am

Having a break from painting. Instead, been doing some crucial admin and have spent ages looking for the stapler. Eventually found it inside a mug in Tim's study. I have no idea what it was doing in there, but that's where it was Lord. Plus, this particular mug has been there for ages, however I've resisted tidying it away to teach Tim a lesson and show him that I'm the only person in our household who tirelessly tidies the mugs away and not him. He hasn't noticed, thereby proving my point. What I find astonishing is the amount of times in life I need a stapler anyway Lord, and why they're nearly always empty when I find them. Spent at least ten minutes looking for the right-sized staples after that. Our stapler says 26/4 but all I could find were 26/6s—thousands and thousands of them. Why have we got those, when they're not the ones we need? Eventually found some 26/4s, only then they got jammed. Wasted about ten, then stapled my thumb three times before getting anywhere. *A sure sign of the fallenness of this world Lord if ever we needed one!* I hope there are no staples in heaven Lord.

Other things I hope aren't in heaven:

Sisters in their infuriating, unsaved, earthly form

Daytime TV

TV

Dirty mugs

Forgotten packed lunches

Crocs

Synthetic cakes

Incorrectly used apostrophes

Blaspheming parrots

KAROLA WOODS

Despot hairdressers

Wasps (occasional 'lazy' ones keep coming in house)

Chargers

Coat-hangers (they get hooked on everything)

12.30pm

Imogen came in and asked me why I'm not painting. It's a good question Lord, why aren't I? 'Just because I'm not in front of my easel Imogen doesn't mean I'm not pondering my painting in my head,' I retorted. She said I need to lock myself away in my studio until I have something to show for it (gulp) and that she'll deliver Tim his packed lunch (shame as was looking forward to doing that myself). Explained to be very careful with the fruit salad box, which is tropical today. Sharon fruit (I watched a 7 minute video on You Tube on how to eat one—have included the instructions), a chopped up coconut (had to saw through it with a hacksaw) and a papaya (easy). The whole thing needs to be kept upright so it doesn't leak. (O.R. a zillion).

2.30pm

Have had another painting and decorating booking come through for next week. I know I said 'never again' but it's a large white room and given I painted better after the last bit of decorating, maybe it unblocks me somehow and is time well spent.

Have done a bit more on Damascus too—plus a bit on an old still life and a bit on a half-forgotten landscape. I need to stop now only thing, as I've run out of Titanium white. Imogen said how convenient for me but that she'd get some for me while she's out.

15 minutes later

Imogen's out. Been practising a few more expressions of concern for her in the mirror (am such a good sister) and written this email.

Dear Rapesco

I am writing to you about a very stressful experience I had today finding the correct staples for my stapler.

Of course, I realise having the right-sized staple for a particular stapler is essential, however I am writing to ask if there could be a simpler way of denoting staple size.

Could we just have small, medium and big, instead of numbers that are all nearly the same anyway?

Why not just have a universal, one-size staple?

Never *once* in my whole life have I thought, 'Oh, I think I need a slightly different sized staple to staple these documents'.

Perhaps if I had a hundred sheets I might, but at that point, I'd be thinking about another binding method such as treasury tags, hole-punching or a giant paper clip.

Please find attached a photo of my tear-stained face, alongside my thumb with six holes in it (from three self-staplings).

Yours faithfully (and possibly in need of a tetanus jab),

Mrs Emily King

PS If I'd stapled my neck for some freak reason, it would look like a vampire bite.

10pm

Caught Tim red-handed shutting down my computer last thing again (hid behind door with light off as he came in). 'Sweetheart,' I said in the pitch black, nearly giving him a heart-attack, 'that'll take me three hours to reboot tomorrow morning'. He said it's a fire hazard to leave it on and wastes electricity but he's wrong. Have also changed his ringtone as cannot bear 10,000 Reasons anymore. It's now the theme music to 24.

Friday 10 September

Computer took ages to reboot this morning—Tim *still* managed to switch it off last night (not sure when as have been watching him like a hawk).

While Imogen had an endless shower, read five chapters of Luke (very long) and put all our cookery books and travel books into alphabetical order. Tim says I only tidy this way when I don't feel in control. He's right, I don't. I bet 99% of cleaning up and down the country only gets done because someone doesn't feel in control.

Lord, please, *please*, help me paint.

On the radio, heard that astronauts give one another gifts when they go to outer space. Wonder what they give? A Milky Way? A Mars, or a Galaxy? Personally, I think a pair of socks would be good. They're light, handy and relatively non-perishable. Imagine them trying to get on a sock over one of those big boots though? They could flick a really important switch. 'Houston we have a problem. No, it isn't the Russians—or the Chinese. We just flicked abort while putting on a sock'.

4pm

Went to town with Imogen again, starting with M&S. While we were in the car, she said she had heard me praying in tongues while she was in the shower and wondered what it was (said it sounded like crazy babbling and was I in a trance). I said it wasn't crazy babbling, it was the Holy Spirit praying His prayers (probably for her) through me, and that it was a spiritual weapon Christians use when words fail and we need to battle it out in the heavenlies. Feeling bold, I also said I pray in tongues when walking Pluto around the wood and I'm not in a trance but it's a gift I wouldn't be without, along with fasting (which I don't do very often). To think Lord I put my stomach before my sister's salvation and lots of other things.

While Imogen went off to look at the hosiery, I quickly went off to the chips section (story of my life). Imogen bought three pairs of tights and a necklace in the time I was away and she was chatted up by the young guy on the till (story of *her* life).

Next it was Holland and Barrett where somehow I managed to spend over £50. I only went in to buy some dried fruit so I can make Tim his granola. Got some chicory for myself (am hooked on the stuff, although not sure what I am addicted to really as it's totally caffeine free) and some of those weird pink goji berries all the way from China. Apparently, they're one of the healthiest things in the world. They say that if you eat a tonne of these every day for the rest of your life, you live an extra week. Also got two bags of chia seeds (also absurdly healthy), some almonds and cashews, some packets of short grain brown rice that I adore, heaps of herbal tea, some tea-tree oil deodorant and some sultanas. My shopping basket was so full, stuff kept sliding off. Imogen got some weird-looking dry soya chunks that spring into life when you add water.

As we paid, the assistant gave me a promotional sachet of beetroot gel. Without further ado, I bit off the corner and squirted it all into my mouth. It was so disgusting, it was like having a thousand beetroots in my mouth, all at once. Apparently, if I'd diluted it with water, it would have tasted really nice, but I only read that on the sachet when it was too late.

Good thing: After H&B, resisted Lakeland and Cath Kidston but then we ended up in the Nike Factory Outlet. Got new gym top (size large as Lycra is very unforgiving on spare tyres) and some trainers (total impulse buy). Trendy meshing finish, but poor arch support so I will need to take them back. They basically look a bit like a couple of shoe-shaped nylon tea-bags.

After that, I saw Alison, the senior pastor's wife, leaving All Saints (good place for a pastor's wife to shop). She can't have got anything though as apart from her handbag, she was empty-handed. We then followed her to Debenhams where we watched her browse in Whistles, Ted Baker and Karen Millen where she poured over some dark denim drainpipes for a very long time. (I've tried to shop at Karen Millen's but the clothing there doesn't suit me. Once I tried on a semi-metallic tunic top and I felt like a knight in ill-fitting chainmail). Alison didn't buy anything there either. To be honest, I'd have followed her some more but Imogen said I was behaving like a stalker.

Instead, we zipped to B&Q to get the green paint that will make me never want to sit in our lounge ever again. Once I was stood there though, before all the rows and rows of paint, I started to get a headache. Dulux green, Crown green… vinyl silk and matt… they all started blurring into one.

Found the right awful green in the end then felt myself go all weak, like Super Man with kryptonite.

HOW HARD CAN IT BE TO DECORATE A LOUNGE LORD?

'Get the Crispy Crumble Em,' said, 'that one's awful. Tim said the Crumble was growing on him anyway'.

So I have, I've got the Crispy Crumble Lord. You speak through non-believers and I believe we've been saved from interior design disaster in the *nick of time*.

Saturday 11 September

Tim not impressed about the paint. Not so much the colour, but about the fact I made such a song and dance about getting the green then changing my mind. We're going to B&Q tomorrow to sort it out *once and for all* (famous last words).

Imogen's gone back home now thankfully—she and Mark are going to 'have another go'.

Just back from computer training at church. Annoyingly, WGM has parked up outside again. I would *love* to clip the big privet bush in our front garden into a V-sign, aimed towards him and his girlfriend's house. But I know for a fact that if I did, Tim would uproot it and turn it round so it would say peace to them and two fingers to ourselves. Tim says we need to live in peace with other men as far as is possible (exactly, in this case, it isn't).

I would love to seek revenge Lord, only:

A) I don't know how

and

B) I know it's not Your will.

I find revenge never works for me anyway. It always backfires on me and usually straight away. Say I try to beat someone to a parking space, I find I either nearly scrape our car trying to get into it myself—or I find I can't get into it anyway. Just when are we meant to fight Lord and when are we meant to turn the other cheek? My guess is probably not when our flesh is screaming, 'I want to throttle that person—or clip that privet hedge into two fingers'. WGM will have to stand before God one day and answer for his selfish parking as will I with my anger towards him. I need to pray for WGM's salvation Lord, which at the moment I don't give a monkey's about—I just want my parking space. How can something that he's doing wrong end up making me do something wrong too?

The training on the computer went reasonably well. As I listened to Tony talking about the wonders of ProPresenter software, had a big urge to tidy around the computer desk (paper cups and chocolate wrappers everywhere). I resisted and took lots of notes. Tony's so pleased am so interested but little does he know it's just the apostrophes and spelling mistakes that I care about.

'There's one!' I yelled as he showed me how to open up a song and add it to a playlist.

'One what?' he said, jumping (he must have thought I'd spotted a mouse).

'A rogue apostrophe!' I said, positioning the cursor and slamming delete. 'It says 'it's' when it should be its, possessive. And look there, it says 'Praise the Lard,' instead of 'Praise the Lord!'

Such shoddy work Lord, and it's meant to be Your house. Tony looked a tad scared for a moment, then carried on. He said the main thing with the slides is to concentrate as people turn around and glare if you're late with a slide and disrupt their worship.

Good thing: Have left all the lovely completed ironing out for Tim to see when he gets back in. Have sorted it into his and her piles and according to colour, so there is a pleasing rainbow effect running through each one. Have also done separate his and her monochrome piles for blacks, greys and whites.

8pm

Very good thing Lord: Just completed a lovely bowl of fruit with Galatians 5, verses 22-23 written underneath. Underneath have written, 'But the fruit of the Spirit is love, joy, peace, forbearance, kindness, goodness, faithfulness, gentleness and self-control. Against such things there is no law' (apart from when WGM parks outside). No idea how I produced it, so it must be of the Lord.

Dear Mrs King

Thank you for writing to B&Q and for your suggestion to create accommodation for our customers.

The idea of hotels is certainly not a new one. We receive many letters every week from shoppers who are so tired of roving around the aisles for hours on end that they lose a) the will to live b) all judgement and c) have to start counselling as a result.

Many customers have asked us to open some kind of spa/hotel/luxury escape within walking distance of our stores.

Alas hotellerie is not our area of expertise—neither is marriage counselling.

There are already many hotels that exist in your area—we suggest you look online for one to your liking—ditto for marriage counselling.

For eye tests, please make an appointment with your local optician.

Finally, have you visited our website and tried ordering online? This is our number one suggestion to customers wanting to cut down on multiple visits.

Thank you for your custom,

A Bucket

Sunday 12 September

Did the computer at church for the first time today. OK, so I got a couple of slides wrong. Tony was right, everyone *does* turn around and looks at you as if to say, 'What are you doing, stupid, you're ruining everything!' I thought Christians were meant to be nice to one another, Lord?

'How about you guys come and do it then?' wanted to yell back, but didn't. I didn't *see* the lead singer signal she wanted the chorus again—I'm not a mind-reader, am I? Don't want to do it ever again but apparently, I'm on the rota for the next six months and completely indispensable. How did that happen?

Have concluded the only way of not getting upset at church is to do nothing and not talk to anyone. Sadly, I don't think God wants me to live in a vacuum which I would do, happily.

At end, managed to change Worthy is the Limb to Worthy is the Lamb and saw that Alison must have gone back for those denim drainpipes the other Friday as she had them on.

At home, wasn't in mood for cooking, so made a very quick lunch: Morrisons Thai Chicken soup (nice and spicy with decent bits of chicken in it). Added a dollop of microwave brown sticky rice for some carbohydrate, then felt it needed greens, so chopped up a courgette and microwaved that, then still felt it needed a little something, so made a fried egg.

Served it in the posh, wide, middle class, white bowls: the soup, the rice and the veg and then the egg on top (put the egg on the edge so it was separate from the soup). Unfortunately, as we started eating it, our yolks broke and dribbled down into the soup like a bonsai-yolk waterfall. I have to say, I rather enjoyed it. I said, 'Tim, don't you think it works, in a sort of weird, Asian-fusion-way?' He replied, 'In an Asian-mixed-with-the-first-week-of-Master-Chef-when-the-chaff-is-still-in-with-the-wheat way, yes'.

Didn't get offended as Tim was the only person who didn't turn around when messed up on the computer.

Weird thing: Think am going off tea Lord—it's just so boring. Am definitely better at making it though, although could be better at making it more promptly. Often, I promise Tim a cup of tea then don't make it for at least an hour because am so busy doing other things (no idea what).

Ridiculous thing: My new gym top has the world's most stupid label in it: a massive thick clump of nylon strips. It's impossible to actually find anything useful on it like what the temperature you need to wash it at. Instead, everything I don't need to know is there written in about fifty languages in the tiniest of print. What was wrong with the single label we had before? I know everything's global now and anyone in the world from Qatar to Mexico could buy this top, but isn't this why we had symbols invented, to bypass language?

Dear Holland & Barrett

I just wanted to write and let you know what a wonderful shopping experience I had recently in one of your lovely stores.

Nothing extraordinary happened, it was just an ordinary visit, but one I thoroughly enjoyed for that very reason.

I love the way you haven't changed your branding over the years—it's exactly the same—the same font, the same green colour, the same everything. Some would call it laziness but I think it's a bastion of stability in the ever turbulent ocean of health food retail.

True, I did overfill my basket and dropped several things in a sort of trail throughout the store, but one of your dedicated staff picked everything up behind me, also fetching a second basket.

I am a very happy customer and hope you never change anything, now or ever.

Yours sincerely

Mrs Emily King

Good or maybe bad thing: Didn't get to B&Q in the end. Tim was fiddling with his bike and I was fiddling generally.

Monday 13 September

7pm

Whose bright idea was it, agreeing to paint someone's house? The room's only covered in swirling thick Artex Lord, the ceilings, the walls, everything! Plus it's 7 metres long by 4 metres wide!

I thought I'd be done in a day, but looking at it, I'm going to be there at least two. No wonder they bit my hand off for £150! Next time, if there ever is a next time, I must ask for the dimensions of room before agreeing a price. And ask if Artex is involved and if it is, run a mile. Feel like an utter idiot*.

*CORRECTION: I must not proclaim that am an idiot—I am a *Child of God.* Was simply behaving in an *idiotic way.*

Will never moan about being an artist ever again.

Told Tim about decorating job (hadn't told him about this one but had paint in hair that couldn't hide anymore). He said I'm not insured to go and paint people's houses. What if I go flying? Or break something, or get paint all over the carpet? I never thought of that.

Half an hour later...

Just made some pasta. As if I haven't done enough work today. Whenever I make pasta I always say, 'That's the last time in my whole life I'm ever making pasta'. But it never is. It's as if I'm in some kind of pasta-making-bondage that I can't break free from. I guess I always wind up thinking, 'Isn't adding an egg to some flour and then rolling and cutting it out into thin strips really easy? Won't it be a nice thing to do after painting horrid Artex all day?' Nearly cracked the granite table top while trying to clamp the authentic Italian pasta machine onto it (bet mamas in Italy never have this problem, bet they attach it and leave it there for the rest of their lives). The thing then slipped and hurtled to the floor, nearly smashing a tile. Once attached, I only managed to misjudge the machine-setting (started off too narrow) and my lump of pasta dough refused to go through it, making me and the handle fly off across the room. In future, I must give the dough enough time to rest too (to be honest, feel act

Tuesday 14 September

Tim has got man flu. Am in full blown Florence Nightingale mode, caring for his every need. (O.R. 100). He's just emerged from the bedroom, pale and forlorn, calling for Lemsip. The only sachets we have left are about three years out of date, but I've given them to him anyway.

Hope I do not get his cold Lord. Am sleeping in the other room to avoid his germs.

Bad thing: Just caught Tim leaving his Crocs in a let's-kill-Emily-location, by the kitchen step. Why-o-why aren't they tidied away or on his feet? I'm either falling over them, or he's roaming around, asking where they are. I don't know why he feels he has to take them off before going in the lounge. It's not as if he goes pig-farming in them, is it? If I hadn't stopped him, I would have gone flying over them at some point and nearly killed myself (basically the gym changing room all over again). At this rate, am going to need to wear crampons to get around my own home as it's too dangerous to walk across the floor!

Wednesday 15 September

Still painting this person's wretched room Lord. Artex is so absorbent, it takes about five swipes of a roller instead of one.

Told them that I wasn't insured against accident or death (and that was very accident prone) but they didn't seem bothered. They acted as if the problem would be mine not theirs.

Why didn't I talk to Tim about it first? He'd have made me think.

Note to self: Always ask advice from someone sane and godly before taking on madcap idea.

Although wise moment: Sometimes I think being with Tim has made me *stop* thinking, actually. I'll ask him the most trivial things like, 'Shall I wear these shoes, hon?' Or, 'Shall I have this biscuit?

Ways Tim has trained me and ways I have trained him:

A) He's trained me to look after him when he's ill and I've trained myself not to be ill for too long.

B) He's got me to hate Tesco and Belvita apricot biscuits and I've poisoned his mind against the programme Grand Designs.

C) He has got me to like parsnips and chocolate with mint—though not at the same time—and I have got him to like halloumi, gherkins and begrudgingly, mushrooms.

D) He has managed to train me to put drinks on mats. Now I do it in other people's houses and even Starbucks.

E) I would love to train Tim to stop leaving tissues everywhere but instead, I've trained myself to tidy them away. Ditto re closing open drawers.

Good thing: Have decided I want to spend more time with You, Lord. Also, I want to be a more effective evangelist and actually risk opening my mouth, not just praying on its own, Lord. Just how are people going to know You, unless we tell them? Been reading Practising the Presence of God by Brother Lawrence who was able do the washing up, the weeding and many other domestic chores all while sitting at the Lord's feet. Of late, feel the Lord does not want me to rush around like a headless chicken but be like Brother Lawrence and behold Him whether am sat listening to Tim blowing his nose, or worrying about starting to blow mine, or monitoring the contents of the dustpan.

Bad thing: Got even more paint in my hair today. Either that or am going grey (entirely likely).

Thursday 16 September

7pm

Praise the Lord! The Artex job is finished with no major disasters, breakages, spillages, deaths or falls—and Tim has turned a corner with his cold. While cooking dinner, I entertained him by playing a fantastic new guess the object game called 'What am I?'

The 'What Am I?' Game

A fun game for all the family!

'The rules of this game are that you must not show the object you are describing to the other person—they must guess what it is!'

'I am an unusual and white, household object that is only ever used in the kitchen. I am also plastic, about 30cm long and I have two lever arms, one of which extends outwards like an alligator jaw (only without the teeth). My other arm has a sort of cylindrical receptacle built into it with a 9cm metal disc with holes (yes holes) in it. Both my arms have a rubber strip on them for grip during usage. I cost around £15-30 and I am for the keen cook and keen washer-upper only (this is because I am a nightmare to wash). I take up quite a bit of room in a drawer or cupboard, so if you didn't use me often, I could really get on your nerves. Finally, the robots from outer space would not be interested in me'.

ANSWER: It was a fancy potato masher. Tim didn't get it. He thought it looked like a pair of forceps—ouch!

Saturday 18 September

7pm

Got up at 5 to make Gemma and Kieran's croquembouche. Never again, Lord. Had intended to practise, but somehow it never happened. I also thought, how hard can it be to make 150 profiteroles, fill them with crème pâtissière and glue them together into a pyramid, decorated with spun sugar when I've never done it before?

1) Filling the piping bag with raw choux pastry was murder. Put it all in, then realised it needed a nozzle in it first, so had to start all over again.

2) Piping the pastry onto each circle on the paper was murder too. Tried piping tiny spirals first, but after watching a video on You Tube, realised that spirals are a no no. You have to squirt the pastry down in one deft splurge.

3) The profiteroles didn't rise in the oven. Rather than being puffed-up, soft fluffy spheres, they were hard semi-spheres that looked like tiny flying saucers.

4) Another sore point, the chocolate crème pâtissière went wrong too. Measured everything precisely, then put it on the stove, but it took ages to thicken. Felt myself ageing as stood there and stirred. Stirred and stirred and stirred, then stirred some more, then prayed and stirred, then rebuked Satan and stirred, then stirred some more, then felt led to use some

common sense and thicken it with flour… stirred again but it was still too runny!

5) Decided to fill the profiteroles with whipped cream instead. Was gutted (wondered how many calories had worked off through stress—probably none as had licked out bowl).

6) Next, nearly had a nervous breakdown trying to melt the sugar. Lobbed wooden spoon into sink in a rage, miles from where was stood. Pluto wondered what was going on—he thought I was throwing a stick for him and started barking—meanwhile Reg starting impersonating him barking. Felt bad was causing chaos and no one was even with me. Unlike the crème pâtissière, didn't stir the sugar (stirring sugar a big no no, apparently). Instead had to stand there like a lemon and wait by faith for a ridiculously large amount of sugar with a ridiculously small amount of water in it to go golden brown. Sang the Stranglers' song Golden Brown as stood waiting.

7) At 9, Tim got up and came into the kitchen. Told him off for coming near my cooking zone. Said, 'Not now Tim, can't you see I'm trying to make a profiterole pyramid?' 'Calm down Em, I only want some cereal,' he said, padding over to the bowl cupboard. Then he added the fatal words, 'Why didn't you make something simpler?' Sobbed.

8) Calmly got out my Heston Blumenthal sugar thermometer which have never used before because a) have been too scared of burning myself with red hot molten sugar and disfiguring myself permanently and b) have never known how to switch it on. Managed to switch it on by pressing a simple button and put it in the pan, praying it wouldn't explode and send jagged bits of metal and shards of glass into my face or eyes.

9) Tim looked on from the other room, eating his muesli. Tried to make a joke and called him a cereal killer. No reaction. He then asked was I sure I was going to dip 150 profiteroles into burning hot sugar using nothing but my fingers all on my own?

10) By 10am had three used piping bags, the sugar thermometer, the whisk (twice), about ten pans and every spatula and wooden spoon going.

Seeing I was on the verge of a major NBD (nervous breakdown), Tim, who is lurgy free now, sacrificed going out on his bike and offered to help (Obedient Husband: 1,000). It was 12.20pm by the time we'd finished and the wedding was at 1.30pm. Got dressed and made up in three minutes flat.

Totally terrible thing: Wanted to wear my LK Bennett creamy beige high heels that I wore for our wedding but they don't fit anymore Lord, as my feet are too fat. I didn't know feet could get fat, Lord? They still look pretty bony, but they can't be.

Other terrible thing: In the rush to leave, knocked over the ever increasingly big aloe vera plant off the conservatory sill onto the floor. Let out the most piercing scream as if had been bitten by a snake.

Wore some vaguely dressy brown shoes that didn't really go with my outfit in the end and drove to church at about 5 miles an hour—or rather Tim did—I just sat there with a profiterole pyramid on my lap, praying it wouldn't topple.

Got loads of beeps as cars had no idea why we weren't zipping along. Even made a hearse look fast and then a tractor over took us. We have a fish sticker in the back of our car and someone shouted BL***Y FISH PEOPLE out of their window as they overtook. Tim shouted, 'God bless you!' in a really cheery way. Then I realised that choux pastry softens with time as the cream makes it go soggy... Is there no end to the type of difficulties that can arise, Lord?

Gemma was delighted with the croquembouche, praise the Lord (would have screamed if not). Smiled at her and said, 'You're welcome' as if it had taken me no time at all. Don't-cook-couple Karen and James had brought an apple pie (probably Aunt Bessie's as it was in a foil container) and looked as if they'd had a lovely morning in.

The wedding was totally beautiful. In fact, if they'd done an aerial shot, the whole bridal procession would have looked like a moving row of meringues, with Gemma as head meringue and all the other little meringues following in a cloud-like trail.

NB: Must remember to get my cone back from Gemma to prevent any new root of bitterness taking hold (have just about let go of the old). Not that I will ever make another croquembouche for as long as I live. (Now I know why Lakeland discontinued their croquembouche moulds).

Good thing: Tim helping me make the croquembouche. We used forks, not our fingers, to dip the profiteroles in the sugar and stick them together. Would have burned skin off our fingers otherwise. Recipe should come with a public safety warning.

Tim's made me promise that in future, when I get asked to make a cake, I'll only make ones that don't require their own internal scaffolding. Otherwise, must buy one. I have said yes (O.R. 10 as didn't quibble whatsoever).

I hereby declare will be nice to Tim from this day onward, forever.

Good thing: Some bird has done a very big poop on WGM's bonnet. Thank you Lord, You're in control of everything.

Sunday 19 September

At church today there was a call for:

A) volunteers

B) missionaries

C) volunteer missionaries

D) mission volunteers

E) funds for missionaries and volunteers.

Essentially, there's going to be a big auction in the next couple of weeks where people donate their services and people bid for them. Tim feels led to do a sponsored parachute jump for the orphanage in Sri Lanka that needs ten extra beds and medical supplies. He feels that for some reason, it's going to be 'amazing'. I on the other hand feel led to donate some kind of painting, perhaps fruits of the Spirit? I feel that for some reason, it's going to be 'OK'.

6pm

Have sent this email to the top patisserie school in Paris (hope have got right one):

Dear Monsieur (ou Madame)

Je write pour suggester that vous makez un change to votre recipe for le gateau croquembouche. C'est tres difficile, et even dangereux.

Je suggeste vous changez the bit, 'dip the profiteroles into the molten sugar' avec vos fingers to 'use a fork' instead.

En Angleterre we appelle that a health and sante risk.

Merci beaucoop,

Emily Roi (French for king)

Monday 20 September

Caught my reflection in the window after walking Pluto. Looked just like a Womble. Sudden cold snap has made me drag out some woolens—my old cream cardi, an old green walking jacket, wellies and a yellow woolly hat. Looked just like Uncle Bulgaria.

In a desperate attempt to try to look more sophisticated, thought would go and buy some jewellery (been wanting some for ages). Have got a nice long necklace from M&S—some

black and transparent glassy beads that clank around on a tri-chain. Only £6.

The thing is, what do I wear with it now that I've got it? Not Womble gear, surely. That would only add to the overall effect—and even I know that dressing nicely is about how things are put together. Weary and confused, had a coffee in the cafe, studying non-Womblish women going about their business in non-Womble gear. I just don't own clothes like these women's though, Lord. If I did, sooner or later I'd do something that would Womblify them and I'd be back to square one. Painted my nails (claws) earlier, but don't think it's helped even though I did a three-coat sandwich. The truth, is dressing up goes beyond coordination alone. There's a Womble trait that you either have or you don't. When I think about photos of mum and even grandma (misshapen woollens, baggy tops and hats) they're pretty Uncle Bulgaria-ish too. Perhaps there is a Womble spirit coming down the generations?

Next, got lost in Sports Direct, as it's just so massive. Had to ask for directions on how to get out. Came out with a £3 hot water bottle, just like a Womble would. My next question is, why on earth does Sports Direct sell hot water bottles, Lord? Asked the cashier but she didn't know.

Then, I went a bit mad in Poundland (quite a new discovery). Asked the price of some tubs of Bisto. The woman said, 'We're Poundland love, the clue is in the name'. Ignoring her sarcasm I said, 'Yes but I thought that the name 'Poundland' was more an indication of value than literal price…'. She walked off before I finished. Examined the tubs to see if they were in date—they were—for ages in fact—so I got six. Then I saw some biscuits for £2 Lord, proving my point about price. Tried to find the assistant but she had gone (probably hiding).

Now I've got the tubs of gravy, am debating if I can use them as stocking fillers for Tim's family at Christmas as for some inexplicable reason known only to You Lord, they don't do gravy (major flaw I know). Once, I took a tub of gravy along to Tim's sister's in Cornwall, only I couldn't bring myself to use it. I went upstairs as they were serving up the meat, veg and potatoes without any sauce and looked at it longingly. 'You could solve everything,' I said, then put it away quietly.

When all this is done, must start on our lounge and get our own house in order. Thank you Lord that we don't have Artex.

Weird thing: On bus home, keyed into someone's highly dull conversation about their dog and its allergies to certain foods. I couldn't tune out of it, even though it was boring me to tears.

Bad thing: Think I may be addicted to Marks and Spencer. It's about the only shop I ever go to on a regular basis. Perhaps I could ask Alison, Pastor Rob's wife, if she'd go shopping with me? She could show me where to go, and I would humbly follow. She could also pray for any strongholds regarding M&S, splodging clothes, using disabled loos and being like a Womble to be broken once and for all.

Other bad thing: Tim screaming as he walked across the lounge tonight. Nearly gave me a heart attack. Thought he was having a seizure, but it turned out he'd stood on some kind of tiny piece of metal (probably nothing). I know it can't have been nice but the next thing I knew was he was lying on the sofa, acting as if he was going to die. 'What if I get tetanus?' he said, thrashing around, 'what if my leg needs amputating? What if there's a shard in my bloodstream and the metal is on its way to my heart as we speak?' Have learned that no matter how minor the injury, I must not laugh in these situations even though the temptation is huge. The best thing is to put on a solemn face and give immediate reassurance that amputation or death is highly unlikely. Then apply Savlon and a plaster.

Tuesday 21 September

The Biscuit Tin

A short farce by Emily King

Act 1

Tim: (opening and closing of cupboards) Emily, we're out of biscuits.

Me: Sorry hon, I didn't think you wanted any. I thought we were being healthy now.

Tim: I know but I really fancy some.

Me: How about a banana?

Tim: No, I really fancy some biscuits, but all that's left is a ginger nut.

Me: OK, I'll add some to my Morrison's order. It's just that you said to ignore you if…

Tim: I know, I know—but we can't not have anything in, can we?

Me: Okay… (Typing at computer).

CURTAIN

Act 2 (few days later)

Me: (Rustling of bags being unpacked) Hon, the biscuit tin is full!

Tim: Great.

Me: Ginger creams, bourbons and some of those rectangular ones you like with a thick layer of chocolate on them.

Tim: Great. Don't put any bread, cake or crumpets in with them, will you, or the…

Me: …biscuits will go soft, I know—transfer of moisture.

CURTAIN

Act 3 (two days later)

Me: (entering Tim's study) Do you want some tea and biscuits?

Tim: Yes please. Ooo. On second thoughts, just tea, but no biscuits.

Me: What?

Tim: They're full of sugar, aren't they?

Me: But you said…

Tim: I know… but we shouldn't have them anymore. Don't get anymore, will you? Next time, ignore me.

Me: OK. It's just that you've said that before…

Tim: Well I really mean it this time. We spend all this time saying we want to be healthy—and then we keep on having sugar.

Me: Ok then. Let's finish these and I won't get anymore, ever again.

Tim: Great.

Me: Great.

(Repeat for eternity or until audience is beating their head against the wall).

THE END

Thursday 23 September

10.30am

Where does the time go? I've been up three hours and am only just about to start on Gemma and Kieran's wedding painting that they want me to do. Tim on the other hand has been at his desk since 8.30. How does he do it? I've been up much longer than him but I still haven't so much as set foot in my studio. Instead, I've been up and down the stairs a thousand times and at least one of those times I forgot what I went up for. I've also put a hundred things away, changed the tea towels, sorted out the ironing, put out the bins, put on a wash, hoovered, wiped down the surfaces, swept the floor, walked and fed Pluto, planned lunch and dinner and done an online shop. (And people wonder what I do all day).

I know that the minute I start working, Tim will be ready for a break and he will knock on my door 'to see how things are going' and be gobsmacked to see that I've only just started. Must put this wash out, then have breakfast, then start working.

10 minutes later

Washing out, finally. Had to climb into the duvet case to retrieve a sock that had got in there. I really wish Satan would leave me alone Lord.

Bad thing: To cap it all, just squirted myself in my eye with a grapefruit. Thankfully, had my reading glasses on so it just went on the lens. Then, (and what are the chances of this happening Lord) squirted myself again immediately afterwards (glasses still on). The second squirt landed higher, on my right eyebrow mainly, but then ran down and diffused downwards towards my eyeball in a Brownian motion way, so that I felt a sort of gaseous citrus dispersion occurring all around my eyeball. I basically had to take off my glasses to liberate my eye area of trapped grapefruit gas. Where will it all end, Lord?

7pm

All in all, not a productive day.

Tim has set up his Virgin Money Giving page for his jump for 5 December. Talk about being organised. It's months away.

Who does he think is going to sponsor him now? (Me, probably).

Good thing: Am drinking heaps of water. Tim's been calling me the Camel of the North—I see a glass of water and throw it down my throat (soon it could become a party trick).

Bad thing: Can't hide anything from Tim. Was still hungry after dinner so tried to have a banana and a Go Ahead bar in secret. Tim found out even though he was in his study and I was eating really quietly. Yes, I did snap the banana off the bunch rather loudly and maybe the aroma of it wafted through, but he must have ears like satellite dishes.

Sunday 26 September

1pm

Have sponsored Tim to get the ball rolling (£50). He's got weeks and weeks now to amass a small fortune.

Auction mentioned again at church. Had spat with Pauline, who was sat next to me. We were about ten minutes into worship when she jabbed me on the shoulder to ask if she could get past me to go to the toilet. Imagine that happening before the throne in heaven, Lord, one of the twelve elders nudging one of the others to go to the loo? Never have I been brought back to earth from the heavenlies with a less necessary bump.

'You mean you've interrupted my worship to go to the toilet?' wanted to say, but didn't. She then looked annoyed with *me* for being in the way. Seethed, trying to fix my eyes on Jesus, but they just kept coming back to Pauline and her asking me to move. Then, before communion, while was still seething, we were asked to repent of our sins and examine our souls. If we had anything against a brother or sister, we were to go to sort it out with them there and then, before communion.

Of all the days for them to say this, Lord. Given this is never normally said at church (it should be really), I felt had to turn to Pauline to tell her how I felt.

'Can't it wait?' she whispered really loudly, 'I'm going up for communion'.

'That's the point,' I said. 'You interrupted my worship to go to the toilet and now I'm in a state'.

'But I had to Emily, I had a tea before the service'.

'What's more important Pauline, your bladder or God?'

People started looking around but I was only doing what Pastor Rob said.

5pm

Major bombshell

Jane's rung about a competition she's heard advertised on United Christian Broadcasters radio about a competition called Christian Artist of the Year. The prize is £5,000 and the chance to paint the Archbishop of Canterbury and his wife for the porch of Lambeth Palace! I must enter it Lord! I put the radio on straight away and heard it too. What do I submit though? It's got to be something overtly Christian. Can't enter Fruits of the Spirit—that's going in the auction. The obvious thing is to finish and enter Damascus. The deadline is Friday 19 November, with the winner announced just before Christmas.

Thank you Lord, for this rocket up the artistic posterior that have been needing for ages.

Monday 27 September

Cher Madame Roi

Nous are writing a you to say that le recipe that vous are parlez-ing about n'est pas ours.

Therefore nous cannot takez le blame pour vos problemes de croquembouche.

Nous vous prions d'agreer, Madam, l'expression de nos sentiments distingues (No idea what this means. After Googling it, I think it just means 'bye').

Monsieur Jacques Gourmand

10am

Just got a postcard off Paul and Mandi. They are in Buenos Aires feeding the poor and giving out Bible tracts.

The other big news, they're going on holiday for a week in the new year AND WANT US TO COME TOO! Thank you Lord for this answer to prayer! Have so often dreamed of swanning off on holiday with P&M and lying by a pool with Piz Buin all over me, cooking like a lobster!

I would even go with them Lord as a maid or porter.

4pm

Painted with zeal all morning: first Damascus, then Gemma and Kieran having confetti thrown all over them. I have to say, am making major strides. Cannot wait to go on holiday with P&M and in between painting, have been browsing online for Piz Buin lotion and bikinis.

Next, went to clean church as cleaner is off sick. Saw a Mars bar near the computer looking distinctly lost. Was about to have it, resisted, then had it anyway. Hoovered. They've got just the sort of hoover I like—a cylindrical upright one with a smiley face on it. I have to say, the suction was superb. Went round main hall and around the computer desk—nearly hoovered up the senior leader's USB but saw it just in time. Then emptied the bins and cleaned the women's loos, followed by the men's which was like descending into Hades.

Off to gym now. No desire to go but still so appalled about my fat feet that must take action. Are there any exercises for toning feet, Lord?

Must look sensational for our hol with P&M, Lord. I've never owned a bikini, Lord, it will be my first one. I must have a stomach like a washboard by Christmas as can't subject my midriff to the world otherwise. (Wish hadn't had that Mars bar now).

6pm

At gym, did twenty sit ups, followed by the stepper. Crucifix-serpent-man Mick who chatted up Imogen in the pool was on a treadmill across from me with Deely Boppers on his head (two red glittery hearts on long bouncy springs, wobbling like mad). Risked eight minutes on the stepper in total. During the sixth minute, when I thought it was going to drop from level 6 to level 2, it went up to level 9 instead and I had to suddenly start stepping at about 500mph. I managed to do it, just, then staggered off to the changing room in a zig zag, gasping for breath. My foot hurts now, so what am I meant to do about toning my feet? I've prayed and prayed and prayed but am still in pain and have heard nothing from the physio.

Good thing: Think have found the perfect bikini for the P&M holiday. Leopard skin and teal. It looks great on the model but then again, she did look like a stick.

Thinking of doing a small one off poster for the gym. 'Exercise is bad for you'. Then running away.

Tuesday 28 September

Whoever wrote the old adage, 'It's no good crying over spilt milk' never dropped a pint of milk and had to clear it up. This morning, as I put a glass pint of milk back into the fridge, I missed the door shelf and the bottle crashed to the floor, glass and milk shattering everywhere—cue NBD (nervous breakdown) or what. Tim came running out of his study to see if I was OK, then when he realised I was, he went back in, leaving me to pick up all the broken bits and mop the milk away.

Tried to honour the challenge i.e. not lose it—and be all Brother Lawrency about it. Actually, would *love* to have seen how Brother Lawrence would have coped with shards of glass stuck in a mop that's sopping wet with milk (really well, probably). Wonder if he even had pints of milk in his day? Probably not. I bet milk back then came straight from the cow and into a bucket.

Tim working at home today, so even more distractions (keep telling myself he does live here too).

To be honest my mind is flitting around all kinds of amazing holiday locations—Barbados—Florida—the south of France. I do so hope it is the south of France, Lord! Or maybe they're taking us to the Maldives? I hope it isn't skiing though—I'm terrified of skiing. Who'd have thought of creating a sport based on one long slip?

Noon

Tried to make us both a pot of tea, mid-morning. Problem free, you'd think. I warmed up the pot, put the teabags in, scalded them to death, then (first mistake), I picked up the pot and swilled it around, making scalding hot tea come shooting out everywhere and onto my hand. Screamed a blood curdling scream, (Tim came in again, wondering what on earth had happened this time, then when he saw I'd only scalded my hand, he went straight back to work—thanks a lot). I then wiped up the spillage and held my boiling hand under the cold tap, looking at the water sizzle on my flesh. Second mistake: I realised I hadn't warmed the cups up properly (didn't boil enough water). Together with the freezing milk, two cold cups, half a lost pot of tea and a scalded hand, it was a wonder I made anything at all.

QUESTION BEFORE THE LORD: Who'd have thought we'd be so hooked on a drink that we'd be dressing crockery in knitwear? Felt had to bind something, but wasn't sure if it was the attack against the tea or a spirit of addiction. In end, bound everything not of God and poured out two cups.

7pm

Made apple strudel with filo pastry. Never again. Eating filo pastry is like eating the Dead Sea Scrolls.

Wednesday 29 September

12.30pm

Am 11 stone 13 Lord. No wonder my wedding shoes don't fit.

Painted all morning, then popped to Aldi because Stuart told Tim they've got some new cycling sunspecs in that get good reviews.

The plan was for me to Facetime Tim at work from Aldi with the glasses on, so I did. I stood there modelling them for him with the label hanging over my nose while he deliberated down the phone.

'They're only £1.99!' I boomed, making the label blow about my face, 'so not very much, and they do refunds too'.

People turned around to look at me (have that kind of voice). Tim didn't want the specs in the end (knew it) but he said that while I was there, could I look for a new pair of slippers to replace his square-toed-ones-from-the-bin (they've never quite recovered from that little episode).

Had a good rummage in the central aisle section where they have all kinds of things you kid yourself you can't do without but can. No slippers anywhere, just lots of Crocs. (They would have done to be honest, but given the present Croc situation, don't feel can handle more of those knocking around the house, doubling my chances of getting killed).

Interesting thing: When I'm in a supermarket queue, I often think—what if, when it's my turn, a big siren goes off and a voice on a tannoy says, 'EMILY KING, YOU ARE OUR TEN MILLIONTH CUSTOMER ENTITLING YOU TO FREE SHOPPING FOR THE REST OF YOUR LIFE.' I know it'll never happen, but I always hope it might.

Thursday 30 September

Just told Tim not to wear a particular shirt because I've just ironed it.

'Isn't that the whole point of ironing?' he said, putting it on anyway.

'I just wanted it to hang in the wardrobe a bit longer, that's all'.

Then thought about how preposterous that sounded.

Went to the gym. Some guy asked me if I was using the massive dumbbell near me on the floor. Said no but was flattered he thought I looked capable of lifting it.

Saw tattooed Mick again. He was wearing a pink and yellow flowered Lycra T shirt and openly talking to himself, Lord. When he saw me he waved, as if he wanted to talk to me about something (Imogen probably) but I shot off to the changing room where no man can go. Wonder if should report him to reception? Guess there is no law against talking to yourself (there should be though—people need protecting).

Also went to B&M. Bought a pudding basin to replace the one I never got back from Gemma (feel like asking her for the £2.99 back when I see her but that would be petty). Also got a massive Toblerone for Tim which doesn't look as big now that it's home, and picked up some circular greaseproof paper cake-tin liners that will free me from the hellish bondage of cutting out my own.

Good thing: I find always I say left when mean right, right when mean left and pink when mean blue. I wonder if it's a sign of extreme intelligence?

Bad thing: For some reason, have started slapping my stomach. Wondered if was acting Biblically—buffeting my body like St. Paul says we should—but Tim says it's highly unattractive and that I must stop now.

Friday 1 October

10am

Waitrose has just been. Half way through, the delivery man told me to go and answer my phone but I said it was my African Grey parrot. In the end I had to show him Reg for him to believe me.

The delivery man was a nice young guy who had not long graduated in physics and was thinking about a career in the army. I could see he was that way inclined. Sort of calm, ordered and switched on, talking about the logistics of bringing the shopping down the gravelled sideway in future, rather than lugging it down the side of the house. Basically he was planning entry points like a lieutenant, only with groceries not arms.

I would have preferred to go to Waitrose in person if I'm honest, as it's such a lovely store. There are other advantages to shopping in store too. Once, I helped an old lady find the Charlotte potatoes—she was gazing about and mumbling 'Where are the Charlotte potatoes?' in a semi-coherent fashion. Praise the Lord, I was able to set her off in the right direction. Another time though, when I was with Tim, I said, 'Prunes are good for constipation, aren't they?' a bit too loudly. He went off all embarrassed (it was a bit annoying really, as he had the shopping list).

Forty-seven days to go before The Christian Artist competition deadline, Lord. Plenty of time really. Didn't Van Gogh do his sunflowers more or less overnight?

Bad thing: Have ordered too many pears, Lord. There's a mountain of them in the bowl, along with around 5,000 limes and a million grapefruits.

Other bad thing: Just realised have forgotten to get tomato sauce. I can't believe it. I've had Waitrose deliver and been to Aldi this week and I've *still* forgotten something.

Half an hour later

Bad thing: Only one banana has arrived. Picked '1' rather than '1 kilo'.

Note to self: Must book sun bed sessions for P&M holiday as so white am practically luminous. My stomach is the worst (not sure it's seen sunlight, ever).

Saturday 2 October

7pm

Tim wants to get fit for his jump. I can't understand it as:

A) He is fit anyway and

B) I didn't think you needed to be fit to jump out of plane, just a bit mad.

Am shattered. In a concerted effort to show support and interest in his hobby, went cycling with him today.

Never again, Lord. Tim said it would be flat, but it wasn't.

'Any road where you have to look upwards is by definition, a hill, Tim,' I said, half-dead. Next time—if there is a next time—I'm going to take a spirit level with me, so there can be no doubt.

WE DID 30 MILES LORD. The annoying thing about going cycling with some really fit is, they get up the hill before you, have their rest, and by the time you get up there and are half-dead, they are ready to go again, but you aren't.

Had on my new helmet, my Team GB Aldi top and my cycling shorts that look as if they've got a giant nappy in them (as if I need anything else to make my bum look big). I had an inexplicable headache for the first two hours too—then I realised my new helmet was on too tight, thereby depriving my brain of blood and oxygen (why do I learn things the hard way Lord).

I also put some make-up on to make myself look nice and like one of these sporty women who look gorgeous all the time. Foundation, mascara and some Juicy Lube lip gloss. The lip gloss was a bit of a mistake if I'm honest, as half way into our ride, when we stopped for a rest for the umpteenth time, Tim noticed I had a wind-beaten fly corpse stuck to my lips. It would have flown smack-bang into them and perished in a layer of Lancôme poor thing, having its wings ripped off as I sped along. I wiped the fly's corpse onto the back of my hand, hoping it would revive (it didn't), then onto a bush at the side of the road and said a short prayer.

Tim thinks the P&M holiday is America as they know we love America but can never afford to go.

He says he's getting thin arms like Chris Froome.

Sunday 3 October

3.30pm

Can't move after yesterday's cycle. At church, walked in like John Wayne. Tim on the other hand doesn't hurt a bit.

They had the fundraising auction after the service—I took in my Fruits of the Spirit picture and wrung my hands with excitement at first—it went for £65. Pretty good I thought, until I found out it was bought by mum, bidding over the phone through Tim! Does no one want my art Lord? I may as well hang up my paint brush and apron *now*.

Went to B&Q afterwards in an attempt to end the Saga of the Lounge and which colour paint to have. It's been weeks if not months now Lord. Prayed in car before we went in. Interestingly, Tim and I both thought we had words from the Lord. Tim thought he'd heard we should definitely get the Crispy Crumble again while I thought I'd heard to definitely keep the green (to think the first time I felt I had heard God's voice and it was about vinyl matt).

In the end, we asked the shop assistant to throw a coin for us like they did in Acts when they couldn't decide who was going to wait on tables. Miraculously, the coin landed on its side. The assistant said she'd never seen that happen in her twenty years of tossing coins for people—so we've compromised and got magnolia.

Tim had this strong desire to make me Mexican fajitas for lunch/early dinner. I like roasts on Sundays so I was longing to say, 'Aren't fajitas just a fancy wrap with some chicken inside hon, and therefore a bit of a low grade Sunday lunch?' But… (area of growth), didn't. I said, 'Thank you sweet heart,' really graciously while silently predicting how hungry I'd feel in two hours' time. Tim likes a spotless kitchen if he's cooking and for me to be 100% out of the way (fine by me).

Bad thing: Tim's only query as I sat down on the sofa in slow motion, was about smoked paprika and if we had any in. I said if we did, it would be in the last of the three circular spice tins in the larder, dedicated to spices at the end of the alphabet. Anyway, as I suspected, we have ordinary, sweet and hot paprika but no smoked—and after Waitrose just having delivered too. Just how many types of paprika do you need in life Lord? (Four, turns out).

I want to do nothing for the rest of the day, making today a true day of rest. Am going to sit still for at least half an hour and think about nothing but You Lord in a Brother Lawrence-type way. Could really do with some chocolate, cake and crisps as I'm always starving after exercise but I know what Tim will say: 'Emily, have some air'. (Sometimes spouses can be so cruel). Don't I need these things for my muscles to repair?

3.15pm

Lunch/dinner still in process of being made. 'Hurry up Tim!' want to yell, (nearly in tears), but am biting my lip really hard. Am trying to wait on the Lord but all I can hear is my stomach rumbling and the sound and smell of chicken frying! It is so true that the spirit is willing but the flesh is weak. I might pass out soon (if you can pass out on a sofa).

5 minutes later

Been thinking about those people who say they eat a little and often. I think I eat a lot and often.

3.30pm

Managed fifteen minutes of contemplating You Lord, but have spent just as long looking for the plastic ball for the laundry liquid again. How do people who hear You all the time do it? They must pray a lot more, or be more obedient, or something—which in turn, must make them hear You more clearly, etc etc. It's a non-vicious circle that I want to get into.

Good thing: About to have lunch (must eat it demurely and not like an animal in two seconds flat).

Bad thing: Tim found smoked paprika in wrong tin in end (Imogen) but by then it was too late.

4.30pm

Lunch delicious. I could get used to Tim cooking. Managed to contemplate You a bit more while ironing, Lord. I too feel You say Tim's jump will be amazing, though am not sure why. I also feel You saying I could win Christian Artist of the Year—but only if I knuckle down. (I can knuckle down Lord—it's all I ever do. I just doubt I'll come up with something good enough).

Good thing: Am feeling led to hone a new system of ironing, prioritising Tim's shirts, as once or twice have seen him fling open the wardrobe in the morning, wondering what to wear. My Primark Lycra T-shirts are the worst things to iron actually, as they stretch as I press them, thereby developing new creases which surely shouldn't happen (a further sign of the fallenness of this world if ever we needed one). Think am going to stop ironing them, as I probably fill out the creases anyway.

Spiritual revelation Lord: I bet the woman in Proverbs didn't have Lycra to contend with. Bet she didn't even iron.

6.30pm

Just watched a Palm Sunday edition of Songs of Praise, curled up on the sofa. Have to say, I love Songs of Praise and am delighted it's on terrestrial TV and everything, but where-o-where do they find the churches they have on there? The ones they show are never like ours. They're teeming with people young and old, and everyone always sings really beautifully, they all know all the words, articulate every syllable, the apostrophes are never wrong on the screen and they all look as if they live in perfect harmony. The choir's perfect, the building's perfect, the roof, the stained glass windows, the chairs, even people's hair, teeth and glasses.

The Antiques Roadshow is on next with Fiona Bruce. I love seeing what she's wearing and the reactions of people when they find out what their possessions are worth. I'll never forget the man who brought in a clock without hands. Trying hard not to laugh, the expert said it would be worth a lot more if the hands were still on. Personally, I like those varnished ceramic fruit bowls that look like savoy cabbage leaves.

Ten minutes later

Good thing: Resisted tearing open a packet of sliced roast beef but just found a box of Thornton chocolates, the kind where every one is a type of truffle. Not sure where this particular box has materialised from but it's currently de-materialising down my throat. Maybe Tim bought it after taking the last box to home group?

Monday 4 October

Why do You test my character in gyms and pools, Lord? Just been for a swim and had another situation. It was the same lifeguard as before who told me to move out of the fast lane. Not wanting a repeat scenario, I got into the medium lane where there was just one man swimming. That'll be problem free, I thought. How wrong I was. The guy in it was swimming really fast, faster than the man in the fast lane even. Not only that, but he was also swimming in the opposite way to what the arrow said. Was the lifeguard coming up to him and ordering him into another lane? No.

No matter, I said to myself, so long as we stick to this set up, we'll be fine. A few lengths later though, he started to zip up and down one half of the lane instead of going right round in a circle, thereby flouting the rules even further! Feeling I'd already compromised by going round the wrong way and swimming fast in the medium lane, I decided to come against his open rebellion and made sure I started my lane *correctly* before he had the chance to turn round and zip back down the same side. (Basically, I ended up racing just to maintain order).

How on earth did that happen, Lord? I only wanted a quiet swim, but before I knew it I was caught in pool-turmoil. I know I could have just moved into the slow lane and contemplated You there, but someone really slow was in there (and anyway, by rights the man in my lane should be moving, not me). In the end, fast man did move into the fast lane and out-swam the man in there too—their problem not mine.

As I left, handed in a comb to reception and shut the door that always gets left open (no wonder there is global warming).

Tuesday 5 October

Home group tonight. We're doing Mark where Jesus is casting out spirits and healing people left right and centre. Some of the group don't seem to think deliverance is necessary anymore, or that it was just something for the time when Jesus walked the earth. Personally, I don't think human beings have changed since when Jesus was around and that we still need it, and how great it is that there is an answer.

Pastor Rob and his wife Alison are coming over for dinner on Friday. Felt led to invite them and they said yes. Am really nervous about how it will go, only thing. I've never cooked for a senior leader and his wife before and not only do I feel I have to cook something totally amazing and 100% advanced, I feel I must clean and probably decorate the whole house before they come—along with buying a new dinner service, hoovering profusely, disinfecting everything and everyone and getting a new three-piece suite. Must stick Pluto in the bath the day before too and pray like mad that Reg doesn't swear.

After a deep period of prayer, have decided what to cook for them, Lord. Scallops in pistachio, puréed apple and basil oil for starter, Marcus Wareing's curried salmon for main and his maple syrup parfait for pud that takes ages to make and is extremely risky. The only snag is, I need a rare ingredient called 'yuzu'. It's only available in Japanese specialist shops apparently but given nearest one is probably Tokyo, I feel it's OK to use the recommended replacement, a combination of lemon and lime, instead.

The house must be spotless Lord, but not in too much of a Martha-ish way and *I must not wear anything remotely Womblish*. Alison is the antithesis of Uncle Bulgaria.

Good thing: Just got a gorgeous pair of D&G sun specs for P&M holiday, reduced from £100 to £30. Also researching suntan lotion that doesn't attract tonnes of sand.

Other good thing: Had first session on sun bed. Fell asleep and only woke up by some woman telling me I was frying like bacon. I've got panda eyes, Lord.

Wednesday 6 October

10pm

Fasted for missions today (didn't have dinner). Tim on the other hand has fasted all day. I went into his study around dinner time with a wan, deprived expression.

'How long have you not eaten for, panda eyes—three hours?' he asked. (I never get sympathy when I need it, Lord). 'I've done all day so I don't want to hear it'.

Went to the 8-9pm prayer meeting to round it all off. Nearly wore dark glasses as felt so weak but thought best not.

I sat at the front whereas Tim sat at the back. It probably looked as if we'd argued but we hadn't. I'm just a front row person but he isn't.

It was a good prayer meeting actually. There was a CD playing when we arrived—Oceans by Hillsong.

Spirit lead me where my trust is without borders

Let me walk upon the waters

Wherever You would call me

Take me deeper than my feet could ever wander

And my faith will be made stronger

In the presence of my Saviour.

Prayed in tongues and wondered what I might be interceding for. North Korea, Syria, Sudan, the Yemen. the Middle East generally, the UK, Europe, persecuted Christians, some of them suffering terribly while we sleep on, world leaders, global warming, slavery, famine, terrorism, unsaved family and friends, friends who once loved You Lord but don't anymore and have drifted away... the list is endless.

Bad thing: While doing our online banking, Tim asked me what the £6 purchase from Marks was and the £30 Debenhams purchase. Said it was emergency clothing (anti-Womble tri-necklace and D&G specs).

Thursday 7 October

Went out for a coffee this morning at Pret where they do the world's best porridge. Got talking to a young Muslim woman. Spoke about curry for half an hour and finally mentioned Jesus. Said He isn't just a prophet, He's the Son of God and that we're saved by grace, not by works. It's our relationship with God the Father that needs restoring, and only Jesus can do that, not us. I even drew a picture on a napkin, showing Jesus as the bridge. She left a bit later, and I watched her disappear into the crowds.

Got food in for Pastor Rob and Alison's meal tomorrow, then popped to House of Fraser to get some foundation as mine's run out. Found myself at the Dior counter, my head slightly spinning with all the choice. The woman there held up this light monitor to my face which told her exactly which shade foundation I needed. She then went on to do my entire face in it and said that if I bought an eyebrow pencil along with my foundation I'd get a free gift (some tiny tubes of moisturiser and a vial of perfume). A sucker for free gifts, I agreed. Felt a million dollars afterwards but couldn't go for a swim only thing, as would have washed it all off (the price one pays for beauty).

Walked around a bit to show off my face to no one in particular, then went home and started cleaning for Pastor Rob and his wife. Got loads to do—there's grime in places I never knew existed.

Bad thing: Found a tub of humous in the fridge that really needed eating. It was so old, it had started to grow a green fur coat. Took it out of its sleeve, peeled away the plastic seal and lid, removed the growth and put the tub right under Tim's nose as we had dinner (I didn't mention the fur, I'm not that stupid). Tim wasn't interested, so I dunked in a chip to lead by example. Still nothing. Moral of story is you can lead a spouse to old humous but you can't make them eat it.

Other bad thing: Why-o-why have I still not done the lounge yet? I've gone and painted strangers' houses before our own!

Friday 8 October

10pm

Dinner for Pastor Rob and Alison a triumph—the only problem was Reg, who started coming out with every expletive ever known to man as soon as they arrived (spiritual battle in the heavenlies or what). Not wanting to cause embarrassment, and while explaining he was a rescue parrot who'd contributed to P&M's conversion because of keeping them awake all night with key salvation scriptures, I bundled him into the spare room upstairs.

I only forgot the widow was ajar Lord. Reg has gone and it's all my fault.

I'd opened that room to air the house after hoovering, wash-vacking, steam-mopping, scrubbing, dusting and tidying. Just as we were about to start the amazing maple syrup parfait that had turned out beautifully, I saw Reg swoop down past the dining room window and into the coppice!

We threw our spoons down and dashed outside to try to get him back. We looked for ages but didn't find him. He could be anywhere by now, he could be on his way to Africa.

Have reported him missing to the RSPCA on their answer machine: a 16-year-old African Grey called Reg, wings not clipped, that swears and quotes Bible verses, often at the same time.

Prayer: Please bring Reg back, Lord—You know where he is. He's not savvy like wild birds—he likes to dive-bomb from the top of the door onto his toy fire-engine and then whizz along the floor with the siren going off, nipping Pluto on the way. But out there, in the big bad world? I find it hard enough, and I'm a Christian.

On a superficial note, Alison looked sensational when she came round—she had on a tie-dyed blue and cream top, some shimmery dark grey trousers and a pair of black high heels with some gorgeous-looking jewellery. I had on a tight black top that has become a bit faded and some jeans that are too tight.

Reg. I have lost our parrot because I was a Martha Lord.

Came back, desolate, to four pools of melted parfait. Then Pastor Rob and Alison left.

Saturday 9 October

Pastor Rob and Alison texted to say thank you for the beautiful meal last night and asked if had Reg come back. I said he hasn't. We took his cage out in the garden last night with the door wide open and some red nuts in his bowl to see if that might lure him back—nothing. Feel like the woman in the parable looking for her pearl. Tim is distraught as Reg was his bird really. As soon as he came back from work, Reg would be on his shoulder, demanding attention. It is heart-breaking, Lord. Tim's upset but not once has he said 'Why didn't you shut the window Em?' (which I know I would have done).

Sunday 10 October

All I can think about is:

A) Reg

B) the competition and how I'm not painting

and

C) how I can leave the computer team at church given have fixed most of spelling mistakes now.

Was just about to tell Tony that I want to bow out quietly when he bounded up to me with a large box of chocolates, saying how grateful he was that I'm on the team and that since I've been on it, he's been able to go and visit his elderly widowed mother who has dementia, cancer, multiple sclerosis, arthritis and cataracts. He then gave me the rota for the next three months. I'm on it practically every other week.

QUESTION BEFORE THE LORD: Wonder what they did with displaying songs/words in synagogues 2,000 years ago? Perhaps they wrote out the words on papyrus multiple times with a feather or some kind of special reed, cut at an angle and dipped in ink? I wonder if there was a rota for that? Or maybe they just learned the words? One thing's sure, I bet they never had ProPresenter crashing all the time, or worship leaders forgetting to signal the verse, chorus or bridge.

Good thing: Pastor Rob got Tim up to the front to talk about his parachute jump.

Bad thing: Some bright spark shouted out, 'Where's Emily, is she jumping too?'

Other good thing: Waved from computer at back like a dedicated but humble servant and shouted, 'Because we're one flesh, I'll be jumping anyway' (that shut them up). There's no way 'I'm jumping too'—I don't do heights!

URGENT PRAYER BEFORE THE LORD: PLEASE, PLEASE BRING BACK REG. Stuart and Liz prayed with us for his return; Pauline too.

Monday 11 October

10am

Still no Reg. Every day we look out of the window and into the sky, hoping that the occasional passing crow or pigeon is Reg and he's flying our way. Am utterly crestfallen Lord (unfortunate term).

6pm

Have just walked Pluto and come across a pile of pale grey feathers by the fence in the cricket ground. *They looked like Reg's*, but I can't be sure. I got a stick and moved them to one side, into the hedge. If I were sure they were Reg's, I'd have to tell Tim. But as they could be a pigeon's, I shan't say a word.

Thursday 14 October

Local art college rang to see if can cover a still life drawing class next week. Have said yes. Need to buy some fruit and veg for the students to draw. Carrots with fronds on, passion fruits and globe artichoke (very hard for novices).

QUESTION BEFORE THE LORD: Why are globe artichokes called globe artichokes Lord, as they're not remotely globe-like. Yes they're vaguely spherical, more spherical than carrots, but they're also scaly and extremely uneven. A grapefruit is a million miles more globe-like but it's not called a globefruit is it? Instead it's named after grapes which it doesn't resemble either. If globe artichokes were animals, they'd be baby armadillos.

Good thing: Just found a traffic cone while walking Pluto in the coppice. Some people put traffic cones outside their houses to deter people parking there. So, am going to put it outside on Friday to deter WGM. Thank you Lord, for your divine provision.

Bad thing: Still no Reg. Tim saw a bird in the distance in a tree and ran out shouting Reg but it wasn't him. I feel terrible. (O.R.

non-existent). How can I have lost my husband's African Grey?

Friday 15 October

Am just shy over 12 stone now. My body won't let go of its fat. Tim says it's all that double cream I have. I only pour a tiny bit onto my fresh fruit Lord. Isn't double cream just very thick milk?

Am taking to eating how they did in the olden days. Meat, vegetables with potatoes or rice and a bit of brown bread. What makes my heart sink is seeing people who are like sticks saying no to a gorgeous pudding or just having a tiny something and thinking that it's loads (I can have cottage pie with gravy and chips and crumble and custard for pudding and think it's nothing).

Just put out the traffic cone for WGM who will no doubt be arriving later. Feel like pelting him and his vulgar white car with rotten eggs (I could do actually, I've got quite a few that are out of date).

Tim saw what I was doing with the cone and says I should bring the cone in as it's an improper use of something that isn't even ours. I said lots of people put cones out in situations like this, to which he said we're not lots of other people, we're Christians. I said what if the cone was provision from God, like Jonah's leafy plant? He said it wasn't. Why is it that I can be holy one minute and unholy the next?

I know WGM is my neighbor and I'm meant to love him, but I don't.

Good thing: Have got into habit of reading Anna Karenina for 30 minutes a day on my Kindle. It's odd, reading an old book on new technology. The characters have better manners than we do today (better than WGM's anyway).

6pm

Just got back from the gym. Tim says I have my whole life in my black rucksack and it's true, I do. I've got all the usual things in it such as money, cards and make-up—however I also have a small tub of almonds, a water bottle, a small roll of Sellotape, string, a couple of envelopes, stamps, small scissors, paracetamol, plasters, Savlon, a mouth shield in case I need to perform CPR on someone having a heart attack, hand cream, a brolly, a cheque book, a couple of carrier bags in case I get some shopping, a needle and thread kit, tissues, a mirror, a rain cape, gloves, ear-plugs in case am near someone noisy, an inhaler, antihistamines, various books, notebooks, pens, some headphones, my phone and charger and my Bible. The best thing about my rucksack though is that my hands are free and I'm ready to face the world.

Once, I remember I had a bit of a handbag obsession. I turned to carriers in an attempt to unshackle myself from handbag-slavery (was fasting from buying them and even looking at them—I basically went 100% handbag cold turkey).

First, I used a white and green plastic bag from M&S. When that wore out, I went onto a bag from Waitrose which was absolutely beautiful—all nice and silky, almost like a membrane (they have stopped doing them now). Then I humbled myself and used a bag from Lidl (probably the most durable).

Supermarket carrier bags assessment

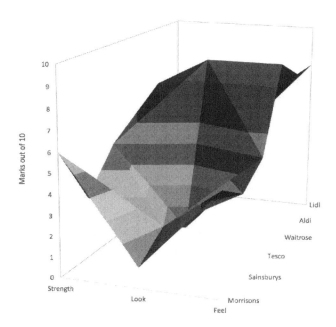

Majorly bad thing: Showed Tim my progress on Damascus so far. He said the horse was at the wrong angle and St Paul's body too small for his head. I wouldn't mind Lord, but it's going to take ages to sort out.

Other majorly bad thing: Tim had another siting of another bird in a tree but it was just a piece of pale grey plastic bag, wrapped around a branch. When he started musing about whether Reg was alive or not, I quickly changed the subject.

Saturday 16 October

11am

Spending this morning on a) Damascus and b) a new short beef rib recipe which takes ages to make. Actually, it isn't too bad.

Have brined it (easy), spent an hour smoking it (unfortunately, saying I was smoking a joint on Facebook didn't quite go down as I hoped it would) but that was easy too. It entailed putting the meat in a tent of foil with smouldering tea leaves, salt and rice in it. I'm beginning to think high end cooking is nothing more than doing lots of little things in the right way and in the right order.

Thought Tim would be delighted with a cheap cut of beef but he said what we'd save on the meat we'd spend on it needing eight hours on the hob.

He may mock, but it's going to be amazing.

1pm

Majorly annoying thing: WGM has removed the cone and parked up anyway. The cone is no longer there, just his stupid white Golf. He has stolen my cone Lord. I would *never dare* do that, not in a million years. I bet if I did dare to remove someone's illegally-placed cone, they'd be the sort of person who would let me know about it, i.e. at some point, they'd come to scratch our car or throw litter in our garden.

Tim says I should have listened to him (true) and that I shouldn't have gone seeking revenge as it only feeds the evil at work (also true). He also asked me if WGM parking there is affecting my life. I said, 'It is'—to which he said it isn't, to which I said yes it is. We could have gone on like that for quite a while really. He also said I should have bigger fish to fry, like spreading the gospel, or getting on with my masterpiece for Christian Artist of the Year, or fundraising for the orphanage and not being petty. Petty? This is about being neighbourly and treating other people with respect!

Bad thing: About to ransack remnant in tin of Quality Street. I'm not sure if I believe in calories anymore, Lord. They are just a worldly notion to drag us down.

Good thing Have had my hair cut again (not the Hitler place). It's all 'modern and choppy' a bit like Pastor Rob's wife Alison's. In fact, I even went to her salon. Hope she doesn't think I'm copying her, even though I am.

Sunday 17 October

Last night's smoked short beef rib totally awesome. We had the second half today, only I reduced the sauce too much and it was almost like Bovril.

The smoking of the meat led to a conversation about what we'd do if one of us started smoking. I said if Tim started smoking I would report him to Pastor Rob. Tim said if I started smoking, he'd lock me in my studio and make me go cold turkey.

Then I said, 'What if I've already been smoking one cigarette a day for the past five years but I've never told you?'

He said he'd know as he'd smell the smoke on me (true, Tim can smell anything a million miles away).

Excellent thing: St. Paul's horse's face nearly done. It has gone through various phases of looking as if it's laughing, got buck teeth or singing the blues. Only a month before the deadline.

Bad thing: Tim coming across a photo on his phone from years ago and saying, 'Hey look Emily, you were really slim then'.

Other bad thing: When your spouse is more affectionate towards your dog than you. Heard Tim saying, 'I love you I love you I love you' in a soppy voice in his study. Barged in thinking he was on the phone to no idea who, but it was only Pluto, who was lying on the carpet on his back, thrashing around, while Tim tickled his tummy.

Sad thing: Caught Tim shedding a tear by Reg's cage which is now back indoors.

Monday 18 October

Tucking into a bowl of grapes with fat free yoghurt and not enjoying it one bit. Meanwhile, Tim is merrily working his way through the chocolate and ginger cake I made for him (I've only had a tiny cube). He hasn't put on a single pound Lord, whereas I have probably put on half a stone.

Alongside Damascus, been doing lots of cathartic warm ups with all the B&Q tester pots we have left over. Sloshing paint around without making it look like anything in particular is very liberating.

Went to Dunelm for the first time today. I arrived in the carpark, delighted there was plenty of parking. (The purpose of the visit was to get a bean bag refill as ours has shrunk). Adored the place as soon as I stepped in. How come I've never been before? I saw a dustpan and brush that I 100% fell in love with. Not the usual small kind, I mean a tall one with a handle. It was red and shiny and only £1.99 (unbelievable, really). I loved it Lord and really wanted it (our current grey one is a bit grotty). However, I rebuked the spirit of coveting and didn't get it in the end—not because of the cost but because all that bending down with an ordinary dustpan keeps me active.

Looked round the whole store: bed displays, towels and bedding. They had an impressive range of Tupperware which I resisted going too close to and a Le Creuset type range which I also avoided like the plague. In the end I had a quick look at Tupperware but only from afar.

Wound up in bedding (lovely display bed, wanted to get in). Found a gorgeous set of Cath Kidston-esque bedding—tiny pink flowers and given it was reduced and we need some new bedding, I bought it. The woman on the till was amazed I'd never been to Dunelm before and gave me some kind of special feedback receipt. If I went online and entered, I could win something really major like a tiny silicon whisk.

Interestingly, they'd asked me something similar in Boots only an hour before (the whole world is obsessed with feedback on how it's doing).

'Just watch the news and you'll see how we're doing!' wanted to yell, but didn't.

The best thing about Dunelm was that there was a cafe in the store. It was gorgeous, like Starbucks, only tidier. The cakes (such as big slabs of lemon meringue pie) looked so nice. I resisted them all and got an Americano with some skimmed milk (I didn't even have the small sandy, spicy rectangular biscuit they give you, but brought it back for Tim who loves them, O. R. 10).

Sat with my coffee and read Anna Karenina, marvelling at how well the Russian postal system worked in spite of them not having the internet back then or vans or people with big red shoulder bags. It seems like characters sent one another letters every two minutes, and correspondence got there the same day. I bet Tolstoy never thought for a second that I'd be sat reading his book in a cafe in Dunelm in the 21st century, longing for a piece of cake, with floral bedding in a bag and some bean bag refill by my feet. I bet he didn't even think things like polystyrene or skimmed milk or the internet would exist. He'd have found it all *absurd*.

Good thing: Have given up aspartame. Gum is no more. Also, (area of growth) it means there are no blobs of gum knocking around the house anymore, gathering dust. It wasn't hard. I just threw it all away. It also means that during the night, I don't mistake blobs of gum for earplugs and put them down my ears.

Bad thing: It was Tim who moved the cone, not WGM! I found it in the garage. Tim wants me to return the cone to its rightful owner. Who is that though—the council or the highways agency? I found it in the coppice, so who really knows? Aren't finders keepers? How can I be obedient Lord, when I don't know what to do? Someone somewhere should write an obedience manual soon, with a chapter on how to deal with stolen cones.

Other bad thing: Have overworked St. Paul's horse's legs and now they look plaited. Why didn't I just leave them alone?

Tuesday 19 October

Did art class with twenty boisterous teenagers (felt like 500). It wasn't still life Lord, it was life-drawing and the model was only tattooed Mick from the gym. It turns out he's a Christian (thank You Lord he wasn't in the nude!). I got all that veg for nothing (could have set up a stall). Feel bad for having judged him now. Half an hour in, some girl asked him about all his tattoos. He said he'd had the dragon done years ago when he was lost, then when he found Jesus, he had the crucifix done, saying Jesus's cross was bigger, and His blood overcame all. Oh how young people need You and Your Word Lord, to deal with this world, to be kept safe and pure and know the way. I prayed his words would have a lasting impact.

Mike said he only exchanged numbers with Imogen because she said she agreed to sponsor him for his charity work-out in the gym for a child's rare cancer treatment he's been fund-raising for (that must have been the day of the Deely Boppers). He'd lost his phone so that's why he wanted to talk to me, to try to get her number.

He likes to evangelise in the gym and pray in the Spirit for people he meets (so he's not been talking to himself, he's been praying). Tried to alleviate my guilt by giving him some of my veg mountain. Sorry, Lord—I really thought he was mad.

Good thing: Traffic cone dealt with. Deposited it neatly by council offices. Then drove off as quickly as I could.

Wednesday 20 October
11.40pm

Terrible thing: Tim's broken his shoulder in two places! All the damage is at the top so it can't go in a cast. No cycling, no driving and NO PARACHUTE JUMP FOR THE ORPHANAGE!

I came back from spinning at 7.30pm to find he'd had put the moussaka in the oven as requested. Was pleased as it was starting to smell gorgeous, but then I realised the house was quiet and there were no lights on anywhere. Went through to the lounge only to find Tim on the sofa writhing in agony in his cycling gear!

He'd fallen off his bike—not on the road, thankfully—on our sloping gravelly drive. He lost his balance trying to get out of his pedal clips and came crashing down onto the neighbour's rockery. He was panicking with pain (amazing he put the moussaka in the oven at all really). I don't know how I did it, but I immediately went into super-calm, clear-thinking mode. I got him some high dose Ibuprofen which kicked in really fast, calming him down. Pain abated, we discussed whether we should go to A&E immediately, later or even tomorrow. Knowing we could be there hours if we went now and that the moussaka was ready, I suggested we eat first (was starving after spinning). Tim on the other hand wanted to get there as soon as possible. I couldn't believe I was putting my stomach before my own husband—but I couldn't face being hungry at A&E either Lord. Briefly toyed with taking him in, leaving him there and letting him get a taxi back while I chilled out at home but thought that would be mean. Instead, shovelled the red hot moussaka into a Tupperware, grabbed some forks and napkins, some yoghurt and blueberries and a bottle of water. Even managed to make a flask of tea for us (no idea how—think it was during the few frantic calls Tim made to work and to Stuart, asking what to do). Prayed we'd get seen quickly and amazingly, we were seen for triage within minutes. I rationalised this answer to prayer, putting it down to it being 'a quiet Wednesday night' but the nurse said that actually, Wednesday is one of their busiest times. So, praise the Lord!

We ate our moussaka while we waited, sitting at the back. There was a TV on with local businesses playing all kinds of ads from florists to plumbers. I thought someone was going to complain about the smell of our moussaka but no one did. It wasn't too long before they called Tim for an X-ray. Eventually, we saw an Indian doctor called Ravi who gave us the bad news. He explained exactly what had happened quite a few times but we forgot because we were in shock. Ravi was clear and articulate but I still had to translate from English to English for Tim as his brain had gone to mush.

Bad thing: Tim is going to have to reschedule or find someone else to do his jump.

Good thing: He's been given a pink, spongey sling that looks a bit like one of those balloons children's entertainers make animals out of.

Weird thing: Told receptionist how funny it was that the fracture clinic down the way had a Dr Legg, a Dr Lightfoot and a Dr Armstrong working there, but she didn't bat an eyelid.

Another bad thing: Can't believe that A&E staff need to work behind glass.

Off to bed.

Saturday 23 October

We popped into town today for a relaxing coffee. The barista gave Pluto three bone-shaped biscuits on a saucer.

Tim's already fed up of wearing the pink long sponge around his neck—it's only been three days. Told him it's ideal for being outside as people will see he's injured and won't knock into him. We got the tram in and several old ladies gave him nice smiles when they saw his arm (Tim always attracts old ladies). Found myself reading someone's newspaper over their shoulder. Tried to stop myself but couldn't. Why do I that, Lord? I have no interest in the Metro, but as soon as I sit next to someone who has one, a story about Tigger the piano-playing cat becomes compelling journalism.

Tim's put a picture of him in his sling on Facebook, saying if anyone wants to do his parachute for him, they should get in touch.

Monday 25 October

Tim might have to delay his jump Lord as no one's come forward. I thought there'd be loads of people who'd give their back teeth/legs/arms to do a jump for an orphanage in Sri Lanka, but evidently not.

He's working from home, as he can't drive or cycle. I keep telling him that if he keeps sitting in a bad position he'll heal like Quasimodo.

Good thing: Cathartically scrubbed Tim's electric toothbrush of gunk while praying for someone to come forward for his jump. Bet he doesn't notice I've done it Lord. That man has got me to thank for his pristine choppers.

Other good thing: Also cleaned TV remote with cotton buds (3 in total). They are such useful things that I can't help thinking their usefulness is not adequately acknowledged across the world. I can't think of one person who has used a cotton wool bud who hasn't thought, 'How incredibly useful was that?' immediately afterwards.

Dear Johnson & Johnson

I just wanted to write and let you know how delighted I am with your cotton buds. Whoever invented them deserves a medal. Actually, I've just looked up who it was, a Polish American Jewish man called Leo Gerstenzang who one day, watched his wife clean a hard to reach area with a toothpick covered in cotton wool and thought, 'Hey, what a great idea for a product, I'm going to develop that!'

It would be fascinating to know more about how he drove the product through from concept to completion. Perhaps someone could make a film about him, or at least a documentary? His wife could also be featured given she was instrumental to the process.

I bet he didn't think that an ordinary person like myself, a hundred years later, would still be grateful they exist and still be using them diligently on a variety of tasks.

Yesterday, I cleaned the TV remote with three cotton buds and sometimes do the hole in the back of the fridge with them too. I don't think we really know the full extent of how we could use cotton buds.

Perhaps your next advertising campaign could illustrate a few of their uses on the packaging?

While the temptation is huge, I've never put a cotton bud down my ear, or maybe I have once or twice, if I'm totally honest. I think my husband might do so in secret even though a nurse once told him he must never put anything down his ear that is smaller than his elbow.

Anyway, I just wanted to write and say thank you and have you receive a positive letter, not one of complaint, as is so common these days.

Many thanks

Emily King

Wednesday 27 October

Tony at church says he'll do the jump! Praise the Lord for such a quick answer to prayer! He says he's always wanted to do a parachute jump and as the orphanage is such a good cause, he's 100% on board.

All he needs to do is get a note from the doctor saying he's fit enough to jump (he will be), and then Tim needs to update his giving page to say 'Tony' not 'Tim'. Simple!

Bad thing: Avoided painting Damascus by sticking felt pads onto the ends of the chair legs in the kitchen as they make such a racket when dragged out. Then caught myself staring at how many minutes the washing machine had left. Can't get rid of plaited look on horse's legs so painting a large bush over them instead (tip learned in art school).

Good thing: Eventually went and put the final touches to Gemma and Kieran's wedding commission. At least that's done Lord. Haven't made Gemma look fat (she isn't) and haven't made Kieran look slim (he isn't).

Other good thing: Crept up on Tim as he was brushing his teeth and poked him on the shoulder to see if he really is too hurt to do the jump himself. He screamed his head off, so praise God for Tony.

Tim very thankful he can type and work at home (he's getting under my feet Lord, only thing).

Thursday 28 October

Just thrown a massive spider out of our bedroom. I only went in to put some laundry away and saw it on the ceiling above our bed. Decided chances of it falling on us in the night were pretty high if not removed, and given Tim is terrified of spiders, I caught it in my special spider-catcher—a large opaque yoghurt pot and a piece of card that I slap over the top. Then I let it go outside.

Actually, I feel quite valiant that I'm the spider-thrower-outer in our relationship. I have to say, my relationship with spiders has changed over the years as I've matured both as a person and as a Christian. I used to be absolutely terrified if ever one came near me. If there was one in the bath I'd scream and run away. Sometimes I'd close my eyes, turn on the hot tap and wait for the poor thing to be cruelly flushed away.

Perhaps my most major spider experience though was many moons ago (pre-Tim) when I was sitting at home on the carpet one day, watching Close Encounters of the Third Kind. Just as the aliens were about to leave the spaceship, a huge great big spider with elaborate markings on its back ran out towards me from beneath the TV set, completely upstaging the film's climactic moment. I screamed a blood-curdling 'I'm-being-murdered scream' that must have got the neighbours worried (not that they did anything) and I watched it scuttle past me, horrified.

These days, I just don't mind them. Now, when Tim calls from some far corner of the house, 'Em—there's a spider!'—I calmly take my pot and card and go to catch it. If it's a medium-sized one, I might bypass the yoghurt pot and get rid of it with a simple tissue. Then I throw the spider and the tissue out of the window, hoping that the tissue acts as a sort of parachute so that the spider doesn't suffer a life-threatening thoracic fracture as it hits the ground. Then it can wander off relatively happy. Basically, I no longer see spiders as aggressors but as victims of their own terrifying appearance—they're running for their blessed eight-legged lives.

Bad thing: Tim calling for another cup of tea and for a hand with putting on his cardi. I know he can't help it Lord, but please heal his arm. Also, he turns up the heating when I want it down and I feel as if I'm cooking. Who's meant to have the last say, Lord, him or me? This is another thing that could be added to an obedience manual should one ever get written (to come under 'h' for heating disputes in the index).

Other bad thing: To cap it all, have run out of cobalt blue.

Good thing: Have corrected angle of horse and made St Paul's smaller.

Friday 29 October

8pm

Universal law: "Wherever you are in the house, there your spouse is too".

Find that wherever I am in the kitchen, doing something really crucial like putting on the kettle or wiping up a puddle, Tim is there too, doing something or other such as looking in the biscuit tin or searching for some scissors. If I then go over to the other side of the kitchen two seconds later, he's there too!

Had to get out of the house so I went to town to start our Christmas shopping—and to get some more cobalt blue. It was late and cold and dark and damp. Heard owls in the woods and the occasional croak of a pheasant as left home. They sound remarkably chicken-like. The car was sluggish, then seemed to pick up. Bought an alpaca jumper from House of Fraser for Imogen (third off). Just hope she doesn't look like an alpaca in it. After House of Fraser, popped into Holland and Barrett, hyperventilating with excitement as they had one of their Penny Sales on. I picked up a big bag of cranberries and wondered what else I could get that was in the deal for around the same price that I'd get for just a penny. Walked round and round and round for ages—in the end I got another bag of cranberries.

Then bought my cobalt blue from Hobbycraft and trundled back home.

Saturday 30 October

One of the things I say more to Tim than anything is else is, 'I can't hear you'.

'I can't hear you, I can't hear you, I can't hear you. I can't hear you, I can't hear you, I can't hear you. I can't hear you, I can't hear you, I can't hear you. I can't hear you, I can't hear you, I can't hear you. I can't hear you, I can't hear you, I can't hear you. I can't hear you, I can't hear you, I can't hear you. I can't hear you, I can't hear you, I can't hear you. I can't hear you, I can't hear you, I can't hear you. I can't hear you, I can't hear you, I can't hear you'.

He can be right next to me and I'll still not hear him. The other day, he said, 'Wow' and I still had to say, 'What did you say?' He says it's my ears, but it isn't, because at the beginning of our marriage, Tim told me to go and have a hearing test which I did (O.R. 10 and I wasn't even trying to be obedient then). The doctor told me that my hearing was so good that I could hear a pin drop in Siberia. It's as if Tim's speaking from underneath a duvet, Lord. If I put the kettle on, or the extractor fan while he's speaking, I've no chance. Maybe I should learn how to lip-read? Once, during home group, I made a point of counting up how many times everyone else said 'pardon Tim' to him during the evening (nineteen). Afterwards, I told him. No reaction.

I then asked if he was still doing his physio exercises on the carpet to help trigger his mid glutes. He said yes and that he was finding them really easy. I said, 'Show me how you're doing them then' (he did) and then I said, 'No wonder you're finding them easy, you're doing them too quickly. You need to do them about a million times more slowly'. He did and found them difficult again.

Sunday 31 October

Terrible! Tony says his mum doesn't want him to do the jump because if anything happens to him, who will look after her?

'The Lord will!' wanted to say to him, but didn't. I can't believe it.

He should haven't told her, Lord, and now look at what's happened. To think she has put *herself* first ahead of all those poor orphans in Sri Lanka! I've a good mind to pull out of doing the computer and see how Tony likes being let down at the eleventh hour.

Popped into town after church to pray against Halloween. So glad our church is doing pumpkins with smiley faces and hearts in them and a team of intercessors in the upper room.

Monday 1 November

9pm

Very good day painting, stopping only to take in a Morrison's delivery.

I've never worked so hard on a painting in all my life, Lord. People think a painting takes no time at all but little do they know these things are done in painstaking layers.

Had steak for dinner tonight, rare. It was really quick to make and so, so good. We have some neighbours we want to try to convert to rare steak as they like it done to a cinder. People just don't know what they're missing, so in that sense, rare steak is a bit like Christianity.

For pudding, it was leftover sticky toffee pudding from the weekend. Have been trying to fine tune the recipe for sticky toffee pudding for years now Lord and I think I'm getting there. Throughout my life, I've had pale sticky toffee puddings, mid brown sticky toffee puddings and I've had really stonkingly good dense ones with black treacle in them. The big question is, how much black treacle is the right amount and do you put it in the pudding only, or in the sauce too?

PRAYER BEFORE THE LORD: Jesus, You who must be the best cook ever, please reveal to me the perfect sticky toffee pudding recipe, so that I can make it now and forever more. You can do it via a cookery book, a dream or a human being—however you like—but please do it quickly. Amen.

Bad thing: Fridge so full can't get anything OUT.

Other bad thing: Tim now saying St Paul's head's too small i.e. the size of a pea! Think I need to ban him from coming into the studio, Lord.

Wednesday 4 November

Tim rebelling and not putting his spongey long balloon thing on. What am I meant to do?

Had the radio on today while painting in my studio. It was a chat show with two American guests. They were booming but the interviewer was too quiet. Why-o-why do Americans talk so loudly? I've thought it many times, Lord, not just this once.

Is it me, or is it their accent? Perhaps that's it—perhaps their accent makes their voice boxes a certain shape that amplifies the sound. Or maybe, with the States being so big Lord, maybe they need to talk loudly, just to be heard?

I wish I had an American accent actually (wish Tim had one too, then I might be able to hear him).

When I get this painting submitted into the competition, I will finally, finally do our lounge (famous last words).

Thursday 5 November

TIM'S ASKED ME TO JUMP AS NO ONE ELSE WILL DO IT.

How can this be, Lord? I hate heights! I hate flying!

He says it will:

A) Make sorting out the sponsorship easier if it's me

B) Save him re-booking it (he won't get a refund now)

C) And… it'll mean the orphanage will be able to take in more children for Christmas and get the medicines it needs.

The worst thing is Lord, Tim knows I'm trying to be a really O.W. and I think he's taking advantage of it.

If he said, 'Em, I want you to do jump through this hoop', for no reason whatsoever—would I, even though it was a ridiculous request? It'd only take a minute, so maybe I would? I'd need to step through the hoop though, not leap, as I'm not remotely acrobatic. And if he wanted to have the hoop be on fire, surely he'd see that it was preposterous—even with a crash mat on the other side, or a massive fire extinguisher? I CAN'T JUST DO EVERYTHING HE TELLS ME, CAN I, LORD?

And anyway, can't people just give in their money without a jump taking place? It doesn't really matter whether anyone jumps or not—it's the orphans that count, surely?

MOMENT OF SENSE: I can't do it Lord, even if I wanted to—my foot still hurts and that isn't any different to Tim's shoulder being broken.

Am not doing the jump Lord, and that is that!

Friday 6 November

Tim seen by consultant Ravi who said his arm is healing. I said it was because I was looking after him so well.

'My husband needs to do a parachute jump for charity on December 5 which is a very long time away,' I quipped. 'Will he be able to do it, do you think?'

Ravi shook his head and looked rather horrified—so I think the answer's no.

Bad thing: Still reading Anna Karenina, about a page a day. Will be aged 411 by the time I finish it.

Good thing: Believe am approaching completion of Damascus. Tim not seen it for ages, which really helps.

Sunday 8 November

Did computer at church. Lugged around a lot of cables and helped Mark on sound get his desk back in order (someone had changed just about every setting possible). I must have really looked as if I knew what I was doing, because while Mark went off looking for some mic stand, Pastor Rob said something about getting him a handheld something-or-other. Not wanting to show I hadn't the foggiest what he meant, I smiled, rummaged around in a box, pulled out something and miraculously, it was just what he wanted.

Alison had a Ted Baker floaty top thing on today but I stopped myself from looking at the label (only just got over last crick in neck). I've already got my hair done like hers too and am on the verge of buying those spray on drainpipes—so I must curb my impulses.

Felt the Lord saying that the jump is going to be amazing *again*. That's the second time I've heard that Lord. *But before You or Tim get any ideas, there is no way I'm going to do it and I know You know that.*

So it must mean You're planning on healing Tim or finding someone else. Maybe Pauline? Or Doris, or Eunice? I think Eunice might enjoy tumbling through the air with her handbag and stick.

Think am addicted to Quorn mini scotch eggs.

Monday 9 November

Tim walking around with 'Don't-know-what-to-do-about-the-jump-Em' eyes.

I put on a caring face and said, 'You're going to have to trust God and I hate to say this, sweetheart… you're probably going to have to cancel it altogether'.

Half an hour later…

Praise the Lord, Tim has seen sense and cancelled the jump.

It's not my fault he came crashing off his bike onto the neighbour's rockery, is it? Thank you Lord, I knew he'd see sense. Surely your purposes have been worked out and he can see he can't ask me to do any old thing and expect me to do it.

Tuesday 10 November

7am

Am on the biscuit rota for home group tonight. I know we've been told not to bake *cakes* for home group, but no one's mentioned biscuits, so I'm going to make some of those instead. Am going to make some gingerbread men and try to make each one look like everyone in the group.

It's *so good* the jump isn't being mentioned anymore!

In other news: Mum and dad and Tim's parents are coming over for Christmas.

Half an hour later

Breakfast time—my favourite time of the day. To be honest, I'm in a bit of a breakfast wilderness at the moment—I simply have no idea what to have. I can't do muesli as it's like eating gravel but the alternatives are:

A) Weetabix (shaped sawdust)

B) Scotch pancakes (too sugary)

C) Cornflakes (never keep me full)

I know I should have porridge or something like quinoa and soya milk stewed to a pulp, but when I stick the Today programme on and make my cup of coffee, all I want is a crumpet or a croissant with marmalade or jam. Mmmm.

2 hours later…

Am hungry again and I know it's because I had a crumpet with honey for breakfast and nothing else. Tim, on the other hand, who is working merrily away in his study, isn't remotely hungry because he's full of healthy seeds and oats which are hard and fibrous and still being digested. He reminds me of Tollund Man.

10pm

Bad thing: My gingerbread men idea for home group tonight failed. Wanted to make each one look like a member of the group using icing-pens for glasses and extra bits of dough for hair and beards. Unfortunately, ended up using Delia's recipe for ginger snaps instead of a recipe for gingerbread men. (This is because every gingerbread man recipe I found had reviews saying the mixture was far too crumbly). Anyway, Delia's snap mixture was too crumbly too, so I decided to add an egg, only to find that it was then too sloppy, so I added a bit of flour, then a bit more, then a bit more—until ten minutes minutes later, with all the ratios out, I decided to ditch the gingerbread men idea completely and use the dough to make plain old round biscuits. These then rose into semi spheres which when cooled were inedible gingery soft pellets that I couldn't take to home group as they were so awful. Had to go to the corner shop to get pack of Hob Nobs instead. At home group no one was aware of my baking plight. Maybe Liz and Stuart's no-bake idea is a good thing after all.

Really bad thing: Tim has seen Damascus and left me some feedback bullet points. I could cry, Lord.

Wednesday 11 November

3pm

Have applied Tim's changes to Damascus and had a bit of a ding dong about not wanting feedback (criticism) anymore. It's getting too late for that anyway and I don't go and tell him how to do his coding, do I?

A man turned up from the National Office of Statistics to ask about our lives. Turns out we've been randomly chosen for some major survey (not sure how we've been chosen exactly, but it makes me feel quite special). It's quite profound, being asked about your life. It's all about how 'typical' we are.

'How typical are we, though?' I thought, after he went. Tim works from home a lot, as do I, and in terms of what food we buy, when the man arrived, I was in the middle of frying an ox cheek with diced rabbit and bacon for a stew. How typical is that? Plus we're Christians, a minority.

The man gave us some A4 workbook style shopping diaries to fill in, some staplers and some matching staples (really rather handy).

Bad thing: Tim unsure about my stew as he has a block with rabbit—probably because he had one as a childhood pet (it was called Thumper).

Before me I have a bag of Minstrels, a bag of Mini eggs and a box of Lindor. How did that happen?

Thursday 12 November

11am

Praise the Lord! My foot has been healed—I have no more pain! Saw Jane in the jacuzzi after my workout—she laid hands on it in the water. When I got out, I was fine!

Why doesn't *that* get into the papers, Lord? It's true what You say, the world's been blinded with unbelief. Thank you thank you thank you.

11.15am

Been testing my foot to see if it's OK.

Have:

A) Run up and down the stairs five times—fine.

B) Walked Pluto without any pain—fine.

C) Done various vigorous proddings that would have hurt before—absolutely fine.

Have therefore cancelled my appointment, saying God has healed me.

'How nice,' said the receptionist at the doctor's surgery.

'Nice? Nice?' I said. 'It's a miracle!'

Why doesn't that get in your poxy newsletter, wanted to say, (but didn't).

Had productive session on Damascus, praising all the way (deadline in one week).

Friday 13 November

It's Friday 13th Lord. I don't believe in Friday 13th being bad anymore now that I'm a Christian. Saw Pat in the garden who said, 'It's Friday 13th' as if she were about to run for the hills. She must have read my 'I don't believe in Friday 13th face' as she followed it up with, 'Lots of bad things happen on Friday 13th, you know' to which I said, 'Statistically, bad things happen every day Pat, so I wouldn't worry about it'.

Told her my foot had been healed (that shut her up).

3pm

Just saw an email on Tim's screen when I came in with some tea (saw it when he was fiddling with the router).

Dear Tim

We at Jesus Loves Orphanage are very sorry to hear that you have had to cancel your jump because you have broken your arm.

Of course you must not jump and we completely understand.

I have let the board of governors know.

However, let us remember that God is faithful, and He will do it.

Wishing you a full and quick recovery,

Roshani Ranatunga

Director

Jesus Loves Orphanage, Colombo, Sri Lanka

Saturday 14 November

I'm not doing the jump Lord! I'm not doing it.

I am not doing the jump.

Monday 16 November

It's official.

I'm doing the jump Lord.

Don't ask me how or why, I just am. I can't *bear* seeing Tim mope around the house anymore, sighing and huffing and puffing—and praying for his arm to be healed when my foot is 100% fine. I don't have any peace about doing it, but I don't have peace about not doing it either. Feel the Lord is saying not to do it to please Tim or the orphanage or for anyone else, but because He wants me to. Why, Lord? To eliminate fear in my life, teach me something, or just to get the orphans what they need because He hates poverty and wants us to look after the orphan and the widow? Perhaps all three?

The orphanage is delighted.

Tim is delighted.

I am terrified.

What if I *die*, Lord? No one seems to think it's possible but me. Tim says it's not a solo jump and that the buddy I'll be jumping with has done 9,000 jumps without any problem. Doesn't that mean that statistically, one's about due? Have started jumping off the sofa as practise but am thudding to the floor like a sack of potatoes. If that's how hard I land from 30cm, what am I going to be like from 15,000 feet? I might shoot through the earth and come out the other end like a human bullet. Have collapsed onto sofa with a Belvita and some tea for emotional support.

I AM THE MOST OBEDIENT WIFE IN THE WORLD, LORD. O.R. A hundred zillion million.

Tuesday 17 November

8am

Woke up and said to Tim, 'Tim, I'm going to have liposuction, is that alright?'

He yawned and said, 'Emily, there are people starving all over the world and anyway, we can't afford it.'

Am 12 stone 5 now.

How have I got to this stage, Lord?

A Snickers here, a demanding spouse there.

My face looks like the moon with a short dark toupé on it.

11am

Checked out weight limit for jumping out of a plane. Perhaps I'm too overweight to do it Lord?

Two minutes later

According to the rules, am not too overweight. Even if I put a stone on every week between now and December 5, I'll still be fine.

KAROLA WOODS

What am I so scared of, Lord? (Dying). People do parachute jumps all the time.

Having home group at ours tonight. People will be able to feedback on Damascus before I submit it. I don't want them to say anything bad though, only thing. (May print up a sign that says, 'Positive comments at this stage only, please— NOTHING NEGATIVE').

Good thing: Have come off Linked In as have never felt linked in to anyone.

Wednesday 18 November

Post home group report from last night

The unveiling of Damascus before home group went pretty well, all things considered. A few people (Pauline) made some ridiculous suggestions, like 'Are you sure St. Paul fell off his horse?', which I graciously ignored. Have they never heard of artistic license Lord, or using one's imagination? Eunice though says it's my best work yet. Stuart and Liz then read out the bit from Acts when Saul is struck blind and we committed the painting to the Lord.

In other news, everyone at home group thinks me doing the jump is a 'great idea'. 'Fear is the hoover of life,' Pauline said. 'I like hoovers', wanted to say, (but didn't). And if she thinks the jump is such a good idea, why doesn't she do it?

'Think about it Emily,' she added. 'If the worst does happen, you'll just go to heaven a bit earlier than expected. Just think of those poor orphans getting dysentery'.

'Thanks Pauline. What has dysentery got to do with it?'

'Everything,' she said.

I know what I'll do. Nearer the time. I'll find someone at church with a cold (there is always someone), and I'll go to sit right next to them so that I catch their germs and develop major flu. Surely they don't let people with flu jump out of planes.

Tim says that after the jump, he will take me to a Michelin restaurant anywhere in Britain.

I said, 'IF I SURVIVE, I'LL BE DINING OUT ON THIS FOREVER, NEVER MIND ONCE'.

Still churning out lots of B&Q tester pot abstracts. At least am doing something with all those tubs of paint we bought.

Thursday 19 November

Tim has changed his Virgin Money page to my name and sponsorship is coming in from everywhere because people know I'm scared. The url keeps getting shared all the time! Paul and Mandi have doubled what they're giving (£1,000 not £500) plus I've also got four lots of sponsorship from some of Tim's colleagues in Brazil. Why is it that the things I try hard at don't work Lord, but things I don't try hard at, do?

Bad thing: Made the big mistake of just 'tweaking the odd thing' on Damascus and think have ruined it. But next to this wretched jump, even that doesn't bother me now.

Things must do before I hurtle to the earth with just a bit of nylon and string supporting me:

Get new underwear

Make will

Find out how can be left to science as not keen on coffins.

Good thing: Am losing weight like mad because of all the stress. Was 12 stone this morning, that's 5lb in two days, Lord!

Bad thing: Keep prodding Tim's arm to see if it's healed. He still really yells so sadly it isn't.

Lightbulb moment: There is Jane though Lord, who prayed for my foot! Must get Tim to her ASAP- he could be healed before the day is out.

10 minutes later

Bad thing: Tried Jane. She's in Spain until December 6, the day after the jump. Is this Your sense of humour Lord?

Friday 20 November

Just submitted Damascus to the Christian Artist of the Year competition.

What a relief!

Repaired what had messed up as best I could, then added a final glint to St. Paul's eyes using a brand new tube of titanium white. Took a photo on Tim's fancy camera, uploaded it and hit send!

The winner will be announced just before Christmas.

Praise the Lord it's finally over.

CAN FINALLY PAINT THE LOUNGE AND BE NORMAL AGAIN. Whatever normal is.

Saturday 21 November

9pm

Cannot say how good it feels to have submitted my picture. I feel like an athlete who has just completed a long distance run. Went to aqua at six, then to the Co-op to get some bits and bobs. At home, noticed the sink was full of hot soapy water and had the sponge floating in it (Tim). Normally I hate this, but… still on cloud nine from submitting Damascus, and (area of growth), as the water looked clean, I thought, never mind, it'll be good for washing up *later on*.

While Tim went about his business, making dinner, I laid the table, trying to hone the exact positioning of the tissue box so that it's midway for both of us (it's been a bone of contention recently as he always ends up asking for it during a meal and I hate passing it over. Then when I do, he doesn't want it to stay there as it crowds him out, so we've been trying to find a half way point we're both happy with for ages).

Tim then vanished—not sure where to—but as I was on tidying duty—given he was cooking—I went to the sink to wash up in the nice hot water—only to find it had *gone*.

I thought, I bet he's only emptied it because he knows I hate standing water with a sponge in it, breeding germs and was trying to be an obedient husband! Have therefore added the caveat, that yes, I hate standing water, but when the water is clean and boiling hot, *it can be left*.

It feels as if we're creating a Levitical law all of our own.

Good thing: Have solved the problem of the positioning of the tissue box. Have got a box each and we put it where we like. Asked Tim where he went earlier. The loo of course!

Bad thing: Don't know what to do with myself now Damascus is in. Feel slightly bereft Lord—and scared of doing the You-know-what:-tumbling-out-of-a-plane-thing.

Monday 23 November

All these lovely messages have come though on my Giving Page.

Bonjour de Paris! Nos meilleurs souhaits Emily!

Hallo aus Berlin! Hier ist €100! Viel Gluck!

Here's $20 dollars from down under Emily! Good on you!

Cześć Emily. Sto Zloty dla Ciebie! Z Bogiem.

Emily, n'aie pas peur, voici 50€ pour le projet!

Hola Emily. Seguro que el salto de paracaídas será genial. Aquí tienes €20 para el orfanato.

Maybe this is what the Lord meant when He said it would be amazing? All these strangers, sponsoring me. I've also got into the local paper. 'Local artist swallows fear of heights and says yes to orphanage parachute jump'.

If I forget it's actually me doing it, I feel quite excited.

Tuesday 24 November

Just found another Michelin star restaurant that I want to go to if I survive the jump. At this rate, it's going to cost us an utter fortune.

Wednesday 25 November

Woke up in a panic. Who am I kidding, Lord? I can't jump out of a plane at 15,000 feet! I've just phoned the company to ask how often parachutes and harnesses are checked and when the last accident they had was. 'The equipment is checked after every jump,' they said—and that, 'they haven't had a single accident since they set up in 1983'.

Statistically, aren't they therefore due an accident *any time*? Just like with my jumping buddy and his 9,000 problem-free jumps?

Am also worrying about that scripture in Job 3 that tells you not to worry, or else what you worry will come to pass. You just can't win!

Bad thing: Me coming into Tim's study to put out a massive basket of damp laundry on the clothes horse. Him saying, 'I'll do that for you Em,' then two hours later, it still not being done. I can't take it anymore!

10pm

Terrible, terrible thing Lord: Just checked the small print re the Christian Artist of the Year Competition and have discovered that it's *Christmas-themed paintings only* —so *Damascus does not even qualify.*

ALL THAT WORK FOR NOTHING, LORD!

I didn't read the terms and conditions properly! I just thought it had to be Christian, Lord!

Tim must never know.

Am basically going to give up art, train as a painter and decorator and go and do that and live happily ever after. Maybe the lad's room and the Artex were signs, and You have been preparing me Lord?

Thursday 26 November

Popped round to Gemma's to hear about her and Kieran's honeymoon and give them their wedding portrait which they really love.

Told her about my idea to give up art and she said that I mustn't (I knew she'd say that).

While I was there, I saw my missing Tupperware pudding bowl on her draining-board. I don't know what she'd just used it for (steamed syrup sponge, spotted dick?) but it looked freshly washed Lord, and I was just centimetres away from it. Really wanted to put it in my rucksack when she wasn't looking, but didn't. I would have felt as if I was stealing it, even though it's mine.

Then I thought, if it matters that much, why don't I just ask for it back? She'll understand.

Was on verge of saying 'Give me back my pudding bowl— now!'—but then I thought about that scripture about not asking for your cloak back, which surely extends to Tupperwares.

Consequently left Gemma's, all forlorn. Ironically, was so taken up with the pudding basin, that I forgot to ask her for a) sponsorship for the jump and b) my polystyrene cone back. She and Kieran had a golden brown tans and looked really happy.

Friday 27 November

Woke up in a panic. Dreamt was falling to the ground and my parachute wasn't opening. Was screaming, then, just as was about to hit the ground, woke up with Tim putting on a shirt next to me, looking all content (typical). Then he asked me to do up his top button as he still can't lift his arm outwards. 'Do your own button up,' wanted to yell, but didn't. I did it up in silence, trying to act caring when really I was half asleep and traumatized by my dream.

After brekkie, rang hospital in secret to check if Tim definitely can't do the jump (it's been five weeks now). He can't. If he lands on his arm, it could make it worse. I said, 'If it's already broken, does it really matter?' They said it did. Dissatisfied with their response, I rang the parachute company to check that they won't allow him to do it either. They said you have to be in tip top health to which I said, 'Well actually, I'm not a 100% myself if I'm totally honest'. Explained that have a mild but nonetheless very real crick in my neck that sort of comes and goes from trying to see the labels in Alison the Pastor's wife's clothes—and then there's my former poorly foot. Sadly, they do not count.

Been therefore trying to lightly sprain my ankle while out walking Pluto i.e. stumbling into ditches, slipping on precarious bits of sludge and stepping into unexpected holes in the field. Have I fallen or damaged anything? No. I'm suddenly injury-proof and about as sure-footed as a Swiss mountain goat being protected by a legion of angels.

Must try to find someone with a streaming cold at church on Sunday, and/or go out with wet hair.

Imogen texted about the competition and when I was going to find out who the winner was. I said I'd entered the wrong type of picture and that Tim must never know.

Saturday 28 November

At gym, offered prayer to a woman in the changing room with really bad sciatica. Thought, this poor woman has been bound by Satan for I don't know how long and she could be set free if I pray for her now.

As no one else was about, I asked her if I could pray for her. She said, 'Yes OK love', then went about getting changed. I realised she thought I meant pray for her in the week, so I said, 'No, I mean *now*'. She said, 'But I'm off to Aldi in a second'. I said, 'Look do you want to get better or not?' Without further ado, shoved her into a cubicle, slapped my hands on her and prayed for her to be healed. Sure she was moving much more quickly by the time she left.

Bad thing: Also tried colliding with someone in the pool gently, not so much as to knock anyone out, just enough to count me out of the jump. No one bumped into me once.

Sunday 29 November

Found a man, about 70, coughing and sneezing in a corner before the service. Thank you Lord for Your divine provision, I thought, I must sit next to him and talk to him and get him to breathe his germs all over me. Then I'll get ill and have to cancel the jump!

'Don't come near me, Emily,' he said (was surprised he knew my name), 'I'm full of cold and I know you're doing that jump soon for the orphans'.

'It's OK,' I said, trying to inhale as many germs as possible. 'I don't mind'.

He then pulled a five pound note out of his pocket and said, 'Sorry it's not more, but it's all I can afford'.

I repent Lord.

Monday 30 November

Paul and Mandi rang (Mandi really). I thanked her for their £1,000 sponsorship gift and asked if they were really sure they wanted to give that much (they do).

She then revealed why she was ringing—to let us know we need to go to the doctor's to order some anti malaria tablets. 'Malaria?' I asked, horrified. We're not going to Barbados—or Florida—or even Italy with them, Lord, we're going to the orphanage in Sri Lanka!

They thought it would be great for us to see where the money from the jump will be going and have got us our plane tickets.

Didn't know whether to laugh or cry Lord.

I was really looking forward to lolling by a pool, but this… this… it will be amazing—just like You said.

Better start getting refunds on all the things I've bought (glasses, Piz Buin, cossie). At least can stop doing those stomach crunches and pig out again.

Thursday 3 December

10am

The sands of time are running out. While out walking Pluto along the lane this morning, saw one of our neighbours accidentally drive over a squirrel—which then panted and twitched and died before my eyes. They didn't even know what they'd done—just passed me in their car and waved, smiling. I burst into tears at the injustice and fragility of it all. That poor innocent creature was only out looking for nuts, yet it was its last ever outing and I could be next. Suddenly I feel very appreciative of everything.

Tim says there's nothing to be afraid of and that I should try to enjoy the jump. *Enjoy it?* The next time he's terrified of a spider in our bedroom, I'll tell him to enjoy God's creation instead of being scared.

Bad thing: Came back from walk and spent at least five minutes sweeping up mud that I was shedding simultaneously. Instead of taking off my boots, I kept walking around making a mess that I then had to clear up. Sums up my whole life, Lord.

Noon

Two days to go. Been battling in prayer about not being scared. Surely the tickets to Sri Lanka are a sign the jump's going to be OK? Fear is the hoover of life as Pauline says, and fretting only leads to evil. By faith am going to order our Christmas turkey. By faith have looked up the recipes for bread sauce and apricot stuffing. By faith will make my Christmas crackers today, even though sticking that strip that goes bang inside them nearly gives me a nervous breakdown. Must put some carefully chosen Bible verses in each one and make sure Tim gets the 'love your wife' one inside his. By faith have completed my Morrisons' Christmas order, which includes five big Christmas puddings so I can have Christmas pudding whenever I want and not just at Christmas. And... by faith am drawing up plans for a gingerbread Christmas crib on greaseproof paper. Wouldn't it be ridiculous if cribs needed planning permission?

Friday 4 December

This could be my final entry, Lord.

As I might die tomorrow, am going to have a really fattening meal tonight and consume at least half a bottle of wine.

Making gratin dauphinois, roast beef and Nigella's salted chocolate tart with Chantilly cream for afters.

At least am doing Your will with the jump Lord (or at least I think I am). Those orphans are going to get those extra beds if it's the last thing I do (literally).

Imogen coming over to film the whole thing for posterity and 'for social media'.

Think need medal that says 'The Most O.W. In The World: Emily King'.

QUESTION: As this could be me my last entry, do I delete this diary or email it to Tim as a token of my love? Or, should I save it on his hard drive so he can stumble across it in years to come and weep profusely over it when he realises what an amazing wife I am/have tried to be? I think I will print it off and leave it somewhere in a silk cloth binder with a pressed rose inside.

Saturday 5 December

3am

Cannot sleep. Am scared Lord. TODAY'S THE BIG DAY. Ate loads last night. Had every last chocolate in the house (house now officially chocolate free) and before bed time, drank what was left of the double cream (have always wanted to drink double cream straight out of the tub and thought if I don't do it now, when will I?)

Tim is also snoring really loudly. Tried saying, 'You're snoring sweetheart' in a firm but loving way but it only worked for about two minutes. Then he started again like a pneumatic digger.

3.45am

Have risen to seek the Lord's face. Have made myself a hot water bottle, a coffee and am nestled on the sofa under a duvet with Pluto and potentially, my last croissant ever, onto which I've piled extra butter, Nutella and half a Flake. Have Bible open.

Should anything happen, have written a letter to Tim, thanking him for being a wonderful 'h', for letting me pursue my painterly dream of being an 'a', forgiving him for the 'j' which led to my 'd' and for never letting me have an 's.r.' i.e. shoe rack (have wanted one ever since we got married).

Have also written to Imogen, telling her she needn't worry as I'm with the Lord and that she should turn to Jesus too, before it's too late. Faithfulness to the Lord is what counts in this life, everything else is just a passing vapour. I remember the moment when I became a Christian. I was at church with mum and dad and I suddenly had the very distinct thought that I really, really didn't want to go to hell. I said sorry for my sins and welcomed Jesus into my heart and life. I then felt God became very real to me, Jesus in particular. It was no longer about being religious and following rules or customs, but about a personal relationship with Jesus, my loving Father God and the Holy Spirit who is comforter and counsellor. Then it wasn't about the rules, as I wanted to live differently anyway, putting Jesus first.

Will make myself a flask for later (Chardonnay), a gruyere and Parma ham sandwich on sourdough with torn basil and olive oil, seasoned with flakes of sea salt and a twist of pepper.

Help me Lord.

Got clean knickers on.

Several hours later....

I'm in the car Lord, shaking like a leaf, asking Tim how on earth I've got myself into this situation. No one in their right mind would obey their husband parrot fashion in the way that I've done, to which he's saying (am more or less typing live) that I haven't obeyed parrot fashion but that it was my decision and I've done it for lots of reasons—for the orphans, to help Tim as no one else came forward—I've done it because I felt it would please God.

Am looking at the houses and lamp posts pass by. Tim saying why don't I put down my computer? I can't!

We've arrived… Tim just parking up in what must be a one hundred-point turn… my stomach lurching with every move. Lord! I can't quite believe it… The whole church has turned out to cheer me along! Imogen's filming my arrival, and mum and dad have come too! Pauline and Liz are brandishing a 'go girl' banner out of the long piece of sheet that's been knocking around for months in the boiler room, probably from the shepherd's costumes at Christmas one year!

OK. If these are going to be my last words in this diary Lord, what are they going to be?

I love you Lord. Thank you for saving me. Look after Tim. Save Imogen and mum and dad and all my friends and neighbours—even WGM. I don't want him to perish Lord, not really. What could be more important than being saved?

Two hours later….

BIG, BIG… SIGH OF RELIEF!

I'VE DONE THE JUMP LORD, AND I HAVEN'T DIED!

Thank you thank you thank you!

I have lived to tell the tale and now that I've done it, I don't know what all the fuss was about! It all happened so quickly, apart from going up in the plane which took an absolute age. We were *so high up*, that it didn't feel real. Before I knew it, my buddy was heading for the open hatch door, along with all the other pairs of jumpers, and it was go, go, go!

Screamed 'AGGHHHHHHHHHHHHHHHHHHHHHH!' as we hurtled through the thick white clouds (then couldn't shut my mouth because of all the rushing air).

Felt like a tiny insignificant speck hurtling through the heavens!

When the chute opened, it was as if someone had suddenly applied brakes to the whole situation. A yanking up as everything slowed down!

After that, it was misty cloud by misty cloud gliding past in near perfect silence—only the whistle of the wind as we floated DOWN TO EARTH.

Jason my buddy asked how I was doing. I managed 'OK' (total lie) while below us there was a patchwork of fields that slowly got bigger and bigger.

All I could think about then was landing safely, and not breaking any bones.

Proclaimed 'Jesus is Lord'—then we LANDED. It felt so good to be on solid ground!

Good things: Didn't die. Everyone clapped and cheered. Am now a local hero!

Bad thing: Imogen has put lots photos of me on Facebook, landing in a heap (and yelling at Tim). She also caught mum running over, her high heels bringing up clumps of grass.

Tim and everyone and You, Lord were right—it was terrifying! But amazing too!

And I've done it.

Sunday 6 December

Have raised £2,772.127 for the Jesus Loves Orphanage in Sri Lanka. Enough for them to get all the medicines they need and ten extra beds.

THOUGHT BEFORE THE LORD: Along with a 22-carat gold, diamond encrusted O.W. medal, I feel I deserve absolution from doing any kind of housework ever again— plus, an endless stream of bookings to Michelin-starred restaurants across the world (it's the international ones I fancy the most).

Bad thing: Tim has found out about my entry not counting for Christian Artist (Imogen). Her and her big mouth, Lord.

Good thing. He can't get mad at me right now. I'm heroine of the year!

Monday 7 December

Midnight

Tim working in London this week. Hope his arm bears up. Pluto being very needy. I on the other hand, am still basking in being a valiant local superstar. It has also lessened the blow of failing to enter the competition properly.

Tim wasn't sure where to dine when he arrived in Euston, so I Googled some places and sent him to some kind of fusion place near King's Cross that, it turned out, had recently shut down (O.R. 1, but 10 for effort). When the next place I found him—a tapas bar in Soho—had a waiting time of 90 minutes (O.R. 1 again but another 10 for effort), he decided to go it alone and found a different tapas bar which thankfully was fine.

Towards the end of his meal I got detailed breakdown of what he'd had: Padron peppers, tortilla, Iberico ham and patatas bravas. He then asked me to text him some travel directions to his hotel. I did this swiftly of course (O.R. 10—although it took ages in the end because of engineering works).

He didn't follow any of them (clear loss of confidence after restaurant failure on my behalf) until he realised his directions were wrong and mine right. (The way I knew all this was because I was tracking him on Find Friends like Chloe tracking Jack Bauer on 24).

He got there in the end, only to find they'd already booked someone into his room and he had to turf them out with the receptionist's help who then brought him up some complimentary milk and cookies. I lived through it all with him from the sofa, with Songs of Praise on catch-up in the background.

Tuesday 8 December

11.30pm

Just seen the weirdest spider in the bathroom, high up on the wall, about the size of a ten pence piece, quite delicate and sweet.

Was going to throw it out using my yoghurt pot and card system but decided not to as it looked really settled. On its body, it had two feelers at the top, followed by four alternating pairs of short and long legs (all of them straight and not bent). Basically, it looked like an ordinary spider doing the splits.

What sort was it, Lord? Was it before you made them scary, or afterwards, when You thought, right I've done enough scary ones now, I'd better make a nicer range.

Need to shave my legs before Tim returns as they look like cacti.

Off to do my readings now and have a pray. There is such need in the world, I could pray for ever.

Wednesday 9 December

Missing Tim. The house is too empty without him.

Have finally started painting the lounge. Hallelujah!

Have also entered the world of Christmas turkeys.

Popped to local butcher and asked if it was too early to order a turkey for six for Christmas.

'Early?' he said. 'You're late. Some people order their turkeys as early as September'.

Who in their right mind orders a turkey in September? (People who want to be sure of having one, I guess).

While he went off to check, and while I stood there waiting with trepidation, I felt as if I was in the turkey version of the parable of the unprepared foolish virgins with their untrimmed lamps.

Praise the Lord, he had one left, which I promptly ordered.

On my way out, I turned back (felt a bit like Lot's wife actually), and said I was thinking of brining my turkey Nigella-style this year (he was quite impressed), and had he ever thought of getting in some food grade plastic buckets with lids on, as I can't be the only person who wants to brine their turkey this year. He thought about it for a few seconds and then said 'no'. Why is nothing ever straight forward, Lord? I'll now have to traipse around everywhere, looking for a food grade bucket.

Bad thing: Passed one of those ghastly shops that only exist around Christmas time and which sell nothing but cards, tinsel and wrapping paper. Went in and bound the spirits of retail, materialism, atheism, paganism, greed and any other spirits that might have forgotten. Then bought roll of wrapping paper.

Yet another bad thing: Since getting back home, have spent ages reading 'how to roast a turkey' articles. The devil is distracting me with cooking a bird, Lord. I could have interceded for half the world by now but instead all I've done is experiment with different online roasting calculators.

Friday 11 December

9am

Tim back from London later.

Went upstairs to check if spider (have decided to call it Steve) has moved (he has). Don't know where he's gone but I'm glad he's living in peace in our house without any problems (I'm glad someone is).

Also dusted away all the cobwebs around our bedroom ceiling (I don't think they're Steve's doing—I think his massive scary cousins are responsible for those).

How do spiders make cobwebs Lord? Do they swing around in the middle of the night like Tarzan on a rope? I don't see them get made in the day. Feel bad for destroying their work, but cobwebs are not a patch on real webs. At best, they're spiders partying—at worst, sloppy work.

I'm wondering what to do with Damascus, Lord. It's stood there taking up room and was so much work. I'll probably try to sell it online. I still want to cry every time I look at it. At least the lounge is going well.

Good thing: Looked up the recipe for hollandaise sauce as am thinking of making it with haddock for Tim. It sounds like a major faff, so think will do it.

Interesting thing: Submitted pic of Steve the Weird Spider to a spider identification site. He's not a spider Lord, he's a harvester! Which really is another word for a Christian.

Saturday 12 December

Deposited this letter to gym reception today:

Dear Manager

I have been a member of your gym for two years now and enjoy attending very much.

However, I feel I must now make a formal complaint about So Here It Is, Merry Christmas by Slade being played over and over and over again throughout the establishment. It is driving me mad.

I think there should be a UK referendum on whether this song should be played every year or be banned forever, never mind Europe.

Also, I think it is a sorry state of affairs when instead of Jesus in a crib, there is a baby Santa. Santa was never able to save anybody, and never will.

I would like to point out that I am not naturally the complaining type. Over the months I have quietly tidied up the gym and the changing rooms, I have closed the main door behind me to keep in the warmth, cancelled classes when I can't make them and handed in lots of lost property including goggles, purses and a comb. Once I even changed a double AA battery in the clock when it had stopped and adjusted the time when it was British Summer time.

All I am asking is that the Slade song is not played all the time and that you remember the real meaning of Christmas. How about Silent Night or Hark the Herald Angels Sing, now and again?

My church home group would be delighted to come and sing some carols and I could provide a proper baby Jesus.

Take the Christ out of Christmas and all you're left with is M and S.

Yours faithfully

Mrs Emily King

Major domestic announcement: The lounge is done. Tim really loves it. Praise the Lord!

Sunday 13 December

Lots of people at church are still congratulating me for my jump. Of course, I'm making out that it was 'nothing at all'.

I drove us to the coast yesterday as it was quite a nice day (Tim still can't drive).

Outings aren't always plain-sailing, only thing. The fatal words before we start any journey are: 'Did you lock up?' 'Have you got any money?' or 'Did you switch the iron off?' For some reason they always fall out of either one of our mouths just as we are pulling away from the house. A disquiet then comes over us and we don't know whether we should go back home or keep on driving. We sail off into the horizon, thinking the door is open to all and sundry, that we have no money, or worst of all, that the place is burning down and we'll come home to cinders.

We went to a cafe for lunch. I had a crispy baked potato with prawns in Marie Rose sauce. Tim had a crab sandwich. I tried a bit of his but as soon as I bit into it, I was immersed in 100% crabdom. 'It's really, really, really, really crabby!' I cried, rather horrified.

'Don't say that,' he replied. 'I was really looking forward to my locally-sourced, chilli and lime crab and you're tainting the experience'.

Felt really bad after that. Was reminded of the verse in James that says you can't have both clean water and dirty water coming out of the same stream. I didn't know I had a stream of crab negativity in me Lord. Wished could rewind the clock and say it was deliciously sea-like and uniquely crabby in a really jovial and ecstatic way, but couldn't.

We then walked Pluto on the beach, lovely to an extent, only Pluto doesn't like water and wonders where on earth we're taking him. The tide was out as we strolled along hand in hand. Tim always wants to walk out towards the sea for miles, I always want to walk back in. If someone did an aerial shot of our coastal walks, it would be a zigzag.

Afterwards, we went to a fish and chip shop and got fish and chips for two and a fried sausage for Pluto. We had to wait for it to cool down before we could give it to him. He, of course, didn't understand this and saw the wait as pure cruelty and went bananas (wonder if I do the same with God). I had to go into the chip shop and get them to chop it up so that it would cool more quickly.

I popped to Aldi after we got back, dropping Tim and Pluto at home first. I only meant to get some fruit and veg but came out with a frying pan, four steaks and pots and pots of fat free yoghurt which I've grown to hate. I felt like a really good Christian as I let two people go in front of me (they only had about three things each).

Bad thing as was leaving: Saw an empty lager can in the middle of the carpark. Picked it up but couldn't find a bin, so left it standing by the trolley of plants. A woman saw me doing this and by her look of disgust, she obviously thought that the can was mine. I therefore picked it back up with big disgusted sweeping movements, to show her it wasn't mine—and brought it into the car. Unfortunately, this then not only made it look like the litter was mine after all, it made me look like a drink-driver too. To cap it all, as I drove off, I saw the bin—obscured by some plant trolleys—but by then, I'd had enough. (Moral of story is—you cannot win but at least God sees).

Monday 14 December

MYSTERY BEFORE THE LORD: Just found a blank postcard of that whacky castle, Neuschwanstein, in Bavaria. No idea how we have this as we've never been there—but no one can have sent it as it's not filled in.

Have therefore suggested we go there one day, just so we can send it to someone.

PRAYER BEFORE THE LORD: We need to do our Christmas cards. Have put out different piles on the table with pens and envelopes, so Tim can see that I mean business. I hope he doesn't write a short essay in each one like he normally does. I motor through mine so it means our assembly line process gets out of synch. At least we (I) have put our decorations up though. Every year we tussle over whether we should get a tree or not and every year we have the same old conversation:

THE DIARY OF AN OBEDIENT WIFE

The Christmas Tree

(A boring play in just one scene)

E: (tidying up) Shall we get a tree this year, hon? Just a small plastic one.

T: (reading paper) Plastic ones are horrid.

E: They're not. Or a real one if you like. Without flies of course. (I say this as once I told Tim a tiny real Christmas tree I bought years before I knew him had a fly infestation—and since then he thinks they're all like that. I wish I'd never breathed a word, *ever*).

T: Where would we put it though? There's no room.

E: How about there? We could move the table lamp.

T: No. We don't want needles all around the TV. The only place it'll go is in the middle of the lounge and it won't work there.

E: OK. Let's just stick to the fairy lights, the Russian-doll style Santas and the large John Lewis baubles.

T: Sounds good to me.

CURTAIN

Tuesday 15 December

11am

Hi Emily

Thanks for your email mate about Slade and Christmas crib not being religious enough. You don't like Slade? Thats too bad! Slade is like, one of the best things about Christmas! Hey, why not come and do your carols one evening, say this Thursday—the more the merrier!? We can put you next to our real live Santa's Grotto, starring fitness instructor Big Pecs Barry with his elves', Nicky and Shel. Sure you guys'll get along just fine! Pick up some antlers at reception so you can jazz yourselves up.

See ya!

Chloe

Work Out Gym 'n' Health Spa

Mate? Jazz ourselves up? See ya? What is the world coming to? I should really offer Chloe grammar lessons. 'Thats' needs an apostrophe and elves doesn't. She hasn't mentioned swapping Santa for Jesus, which means Lord… she hasn't forbidden it either.

I'm going to buy a baby Jesus, Lord, and get that Santa our of your crib.

10pm

Post home group report

Home group good tonight. Everyone was delighted about our carol-singing invitation to the gym. During the main body of teaching, Eunice asked, 'Are we getting any better? Because there's no point carrying on if we're not'.

I guess she's right. People opened up about their struggles after that, giving examples of ungodliness/godliness in their lives and not being Christ-like. We spoke a bit about a famous missionary, Hudson Taylor. I had no idea he was from Barnsley—I thought he was Chinese.

We then got onto the topic of working on the sabbath and Stuart started talking about Eric Liddell the athlete not running on a Sunday. Have we let go of this too much Lord in this 24/7 age? I'm not really sure, but I suppose we have. It's about prioritizing You, isn't it?

Half way through, Stuart got up to find a book about Eric Liddle, spilling a full mug of tea over the sofa. Unruffled, he then found the book in question—and he started to read from it. I didn't listen that much if I'm totally honestly as I kept thinking about the spilled tea on the sofa arm (Stuart and Liz spill tea rather a lot have noticed, they could really do with getting a wash-vac with upholstery attachments).

Sang happy birthday for someone without knowing whose birthday it was until we got to the name: Brenda. There was a cake and a card from the group which Tim and I signed after Brenda had opened it. What I find interesting about birthday cards is the amount of bags involved in getting them from A to B. A lot of cards understandably come in cellophane (a type of bag), which the shop assistant then puts inside a paper bag at point of purchase. These temporary covers then get shed—but once written, the card then goes into an envelope (basically another type of bag), which is then put inside a handbag or carrier bag (another type of bag), which then goes into a car, (yet another type of bag)—albeit metal and without handles. Just how much protection does a card need? We don't protect people as much.

Nice thing: Stuart and Liz's big, real Christmas tree was on which even Tim had to confess, was beautiful in their front bay window. There are lights on in some people's gardens too. How do people get electricity outside their houses Lord? It's one of life's eternal mysteries but there's never anyone around when I remember to ask.

Bad thing: Have stopped wearing clothes that match again (woolly tights, misshapen denim skirt etc). Womble stronghold obviously back.

Wednesday 16 December

10am

Just found an email in my junk mail folder from UCB Radio saying that I've won the Christian Artist of the Year competition. I don't get it, Lord. I've read it, re-read it, and then read it again. How can I have won, when I wasn't eligible? I unsubscribed from their newsletter when I realized Damascus wasn't eligible, but this isn't a newsletter email, it's addressed just to me and looks really personal. How can I have won Lord, when my painting wasn't Christmas-themed?

They should know better than to make mistakes like this really. If I wasn't such a godly person, I could make a big deal of this and write a stern letter of complaint about having my hopes cruelly raised. Instead, have replied very graciously, saying 'There must be some mistake' and have included a copy and paste of their own terms and conditions.

Have also put 'blessings' in the sign off, as Christians often do that.

3pm

Nine days till Christmas, Lord. Did aqua at lunchtime. In front of me was a really slim woman with her blond-streaked hair up in a messy but attractive sort of knot. She had immaculate nails (French manicure), a gorgeous figure and a sprig of mistletoe clipped into her hair. She had on a gold watch (must have been waterproof), a fancy wedding ring and an even larger engagement ring. Her costume was nice too. I must admit that at one point, I wondered if she'd had breast implants put in— as during all the jumping around I couldn't help noticing she wasn't bouncing about at all whereas I was nearly causing a tidal wave. I thought how can someone so slim and petite have such big and orb-like breasts? I then repented as it's not my business and I don't know what's going on in her life anyway. Felt totally bedraggled and like a full-blown Womble next to her Lord, in my utilitarian black cossie and my 80% chipped nail varnish.

Bad thing: Weight going back up now jump is over and am not going to be lolling around on a beach in the south of France anymore. Feel like beached whale.

Good thing: Made Bobotie for dinner, a South African dish that I've been wanting to makes for ages. Curried minced beef with jam, grated carrot and onion, and an eggy milky topping, sprinkling with almonds—random or what? Ate it while trying to do a South African accent (Tim said I sounded French).

Other bad thing: Did the kitchen floor which we both then slipped on. I slipped while ironing (what are the chances of that happening Lord, I was hardly moving) then Tim came in and in the middle of saying, 'Watch out Em,' he slipped too! Must do floor when people are not in transit (basically at 3am).

Thursday 17 December

Shock horror, our B&Q is no more. That was a twist I wasn't expecting. How on earth are we going to do anything around the house now? I'm going to miss our hellish trips out there that had no end.

I'd driven out there as I want to paint the front door before Christmas (same colour as before, thankfully) only to find an apocalyptic barren wasteland. Pressed my face against the door and stared at the empty aisles.

Drove off and found a place called Crown Trade in the end, on one of these strange, forsaken industrial estates where only tradespeople go, and people like me. The assistant—who was also the manager—was very knowledgeable. The store phone kept ringing with this double kind of ring (which only made it seem all the more urgent) but he didn't answer it, he just dealt with me. I was rather impressed. The bombshell is... retail paint has loads more water in it than trade paint. And there I was thinking paint was just paint!

Paint is not just paint just like tea is not just tea and sandwich box plastic is not just sandwich box plastic. Came out feeling really educated.

Then went to B&M to find a large baby doll to be baby Jesus—got one for the princely sum of £14.99—and crept into the gym just as a coach party was arriving and checking in for the bowling. I made a quick furtive move, swapping baby Santa for sweet baby Jesus (shoved the Santa on top of a locker).

Carols tonight. Must sing really loudly to drown out Slade.

KAROLA WOODS

Friday 18 December
11.50am

Carol-singing a triumph. Definitely drowned out Slade and glorified God with antlers on our head. No one has questioned Santa's disappearance or the sudden appearance of Jesus (or if they have, I don't know about it). Managed to give some tracts for the Christmas service at church too.

UCB Radio have rung to say they've got my email with their competition terms and conditions pasted in—but that I have definitely won Christian Artist of the Year and can I go in for an interview early next week? Just as I was about to yell 'hoaxes are cruel' and bang the hone down, I heard their jingle playing in the background along with other broadcast content, so it had to be them.

I started to explain all over again that I couldn't have won as my picture wasn't Christmas-themed, but the lady assured me the judges felt that my entry was, by its abstract nature, eligible.

'Abstract?' I said. 'I know St. Paul and his horse were a bit 'out there' but even the harshest critic couldn't call them abstract'.

'No, no. You definitely entered an untitled abstract piece, with no horse or St. Paul in it'.

'Sorry?'

'You entered a scape of swirling taupes, magnolia, pale blues and pastel greens. The judges thought it evoked the night Christ was born beautifully. Its ethereal, transcendent quality is a magnificent symbol of the Lord's incarnation...'

I KNOW WHAT'S HAPPENED, LORD.

Instead of attaching DamascusFINAL.jpg when I submitted my application, I somehow attached a B&Qtesterpot.jpeg!

Monday 21 December

UCB Radio transcription

Presenter: And now onto our next piece. Every year we hold the competition, Christian Artist of the Year, and every year we have a wonderful winner. Well I'm delighted to say we have the winner of this year's competition here in the studio—and that person is—Emily King! Welcome Emily, and congratulations for winning.

Me: Thank you very much—it's wonderful to be here.

Presenter: So first things first Emily, how does it feel to be the winner of Christian Artist of the Year? You know we had thousands of entries from all over the world.

Me: (surprised) Thousands—really?

Presenter: Oh yes.

Me: I had no idea. Well it feels totally amazing—beyond my wildest dreams.

Presenter: We have the painting here in the studio. Would you like to describe it for our listeners at home? It's very dramatic, and has a lot of movement in it.

Me: Er... Yes. Well it's a swirling mass of light greens and blues, taupes, magnolia—and the odd dusty pink.

Presenter: It's not just that though—it's a beautiful and powerful metaphor for the miracle of the Christ child coming to earth.

Me: Yes, yes, of course—that was on the tip of my tongue.

Presenter: How long did it take you? Days, weeks, months?

Me: About two minutes.

Presenter: Two minutes?

KAROLA WOODS

Me: Sorry—I mean two hours—no, no—I mean two weeks—no, two years! It didn't take long *to do*... but at least two years of thought... to prepare and build... to this climactic moment of my career thus far.

Presenter: Marvellous. Abstract works can have a very long gestation... as they express the inner person, don't they?

Me: Yes, absolutely. I couldn't have put it better myself.

Presenter: Now I have to admit, I'm a bit of a painter myself—not to your level of course—but what is it done in Emily—oils, or acrylic? It has quite an unusual finish.

Me: Vinyl matt.

Presenter: Vinyl matt?

Me: (awkward) Yes, I had quite a bit to use up. For various reasons.

Presenter: And why all the magnolia?

Me: Well I didn't have much blue—just lots and lots of magnolia—and er... I liked using it—for the light. With a bit of pale green.

Presenter: Right, yes, yes, I see what you mean... it gives it that amazing ethereal quality—akin to the Aurora Borealis. So what was the idea behind your picture Emily?

Me: Well, em, well...

Presenter: You dug deep?

Me: You could say that...

Presenter: These big works of art—they take your whole heart, don't they? And here we are trying to get you to sum up in a few words—when it must be so hard to articulate.

Me: How very true.

Presenter: So you're married to Tim...

Me: That's right.

Presenter: What does he think of you winning Christian Artist of the Year? He must be very proud.

Me: I'll say. I mean yes, yes, he is. He's been praying for a breakthrough for years and years and years and years! He's been so supportive, giving me lots of great 'advice'—and making lots of cups of tea. A few, anyway.

Presenter: Lovely! Oh—we've just had a question come in from a listener... *'Congratulations Emily. How do you prepare before you paint? Do you fast and pray?'*

Me: (shocked) Fast and pray? Er, probably not as much as I should... Er, er... I tend to do things to loosen me up like housework, going to the gym and er... walking my dog.

Presenter: Everyday things, wonderful! God is everywhere and in everything.

Me: Exactly.

Presenter: Now a little bird told me you recently did a parachute jump to raise funds for an orphanage in Sri Lanka and that you raised nearly £3,000.

Me: Oh that! Ha, ha, ha, ha, ha! Yes I did a jump—nothing grand really—I mean who wouldn't jump for children in need? I'm going out there soon, to visit the orphanage.

Presenter: Amazing! And how do you feel about painting the Archbishop of Canterbury and his good wife's portrait? That's quite a commission, isn't it? And what a prize!

Me: Yes it'll be quite a challenge if I'm honest—but a real honour. I did my pastor and his family for a church auction one year and that picture is still hanging at church under the stairs, by the ladies' toilets. All I would say is... photo realism doesn't have to be the only way. There's Cubism, abstract expressionism maybe even symbolism... I don't think the portrait necessarily needs to look like them... *exactly*.

Presenter: Emily King—Christian Artist of the Year—thank you very much for coming into the studio today.

FADE

Tuesday 22 December

We're re-doing all our Christmas cards to people in the village as Tim's had my vinyl matt B&Q painting printed up as a new set of cards.

We're calling it "Bethlehem Night: The Night That Christ Came To Earth To Save Us Because Adam And Eve Sinned—And As There Can Be No Forgiveness Without The Shedding Of Blood—Sinless Jesus Gave Himself As The Perfect Sin Offering To Sort The Problem Out Once And For All".

The only problem is there's not much room to say anything else.

9pm

Only two days before Christmas, Lord. Cards delivered to whole of village (even WGM's girlfriend's house). All I need to do is pick up the turkey tomorrow (probably being plucked right now, poor thing).

Have hung up the wreath that Tim and I made at a weekend workshop a couple of years ago—it makes the house look so welcoming. We couldn't face paying £25 for a shop bought one, so instead, we spent £40 each on a special wreath-making workshop, figuring it would be quality time spent together and an outing we'd look back on fondly in years to come. We do look back on the workshop actually, but for entirely different reasons i.e. getting lost on the way, realising we hadn't taken any materials of our own like we should have—and having a major ding dong about setting off too late. Tim nearly ran over a pheasant too.

Am coating the turkey, the potatoes, the gravy and the whole Christmas period, in prayer.

Wednesday 23 December

Went to butcher's first thing to pick up our turkey. While waiting, I scribbled this poem:

Ode to Turkey

Turkey, dear Turkey

You who cost a whopping £56

Here you are, All 14lb of you

Plucked and prepared

In our home

Soon to be in a bucket of brine

PS

Did you know you're named after a country?

(RIP)

I'm going to call the turkey Nigel. A name is the least the poor thing deserves.

1.30pm (post mince pie)

Just thought Lord—wouldn't it be nice if we had mince pies all year round and not just at Christmas? Perhaps I should set up a Royal Society for the Proliferation of Mince Pies (RSPMP) and tirelessly campaign to make mince pies available all year, not just in December? Actually, I think Morrisons have them all year round, so so much for that idea.

1 hour later...

Just wrapped everyone's pressies. Tim's doesn't need wrapping actually. It's so secret that I'm not even going to put it in this diary in case he comes snooping. He won't though. Tim is the least likely person to snoop in the whole wide world.

Thursday 24 December

3pm

About to commence the Most Important Poultry Procedure of the Year (MIPPOFY):

BRINING THE TURKEY

4.30pm

MIPPOFY highly tricky, in the end.

1) Unsure Nigel would fit into my new clean giant Tupperware, I popped him in to check—he did. Hallelujah!

2) As he fitted perfectly, I thought, great Lord, I'll leave him in there. Then, to my horror, I noticed the cardboard carton Nigel came in said, 'Take out of box immediately after purchase'—which I hadn't done!

3) It also said refrigerate immediately (in big red capital letters) which again, I hadn't done. I'd just left Nigel in the conservatory overnight, with his giblets in a bag. Am scared of giving everyone salmonella Lord!

4) In a major turkey flap, I then added water, sugar, salt and spices to the tub, at which point I read that the brine needs to go in the Tupperware *before* the bird, not vice versa, so all the sugar and salt and spices are stirred in evenly.

Could I possibly have made any more mistakes for the MIPPOFY Lord? Mum says you learn all your life but you still die stupid—she's right.

If we don't get salmonella, die or end up in hospital on Christmas day now, it will be a total miracle. I may as well phone and book an ambulance now so we can all go in together.

10 minutes later

Thank you Lord—MIPPOFY done for another year. It's been such a big challenge, I might use it as an example of a major personal achievement in my life at a job interview, should I ever have one. I think complex domestic procedures are grossly overlooked and should feature on CVs. (I could put Kieran and Gemma's croquembouche on there too, and the lemon and yuzu parfait).

Have now taken the Tupperware and Nigel to the garage—tub-lid *on*—as Nigella advises. (Yes foxes can't get into a locked garage, but I like following procedures to the nth degree).

Bad thing: Nearly went flying over Tim's Crocs as went out—but the Lord had me spot them just in time.

Good thing: Have parked our car outside the house so mum and dad and Tim's parents can park tomorrow, not WGM. He will have to go on his girlfriend's drive where he belongs.

Other bad thing: I bet when we go to church tomorrow, he'll drive over and take the space in a brazen selfish fashion. Am almost tempted not to go to church Lord, just so I can save it.

10 minutes later

Feel Holy Spirit doesn't want me to park outside our house in a fleshly, possessive, petty way but leave it free for WGM as my attitude towards him really stinks. *My attitude, Lord? What about his?* Have the verse if someone asks you for your tunic, give him your cloak as well... ringing around my head. He hasn't even asked though, so surely that verse cannot apply.

Half an hour later

Prompting not gone away. Have tried ignoring it but it's getting stronger.

10 minutes later

Prompting so strong that have moved the car, meaning WGM can park there, if he wants. Even got a shovel out and shovelled away the snow. The paradox of being a Christian, Lord.

Very good thing: Tim's Christmas present has just been delivered. Skittles, another beautiful rescued African Grey. Tim delighted.

Friday 25 December

8.30am

Happy Christmas Lord. Everywhere looks really quiet—no traffic anywhere. Just come downstairs to make myself a coffee. It hasn't snowed anymore. What was there has frozen over. Must get Nigel out of garage ASAP so that he comes to room temperature and doesn't hit the oven stone cold.

There's a pile of torn up Christmas wrapping paper by the tree. Aw—Pluto. I know what's happened. He's torn open his new toy, a new rubber chicken I got him and put by the tree last night. He must have smelled it and known it was a toy. Where is Pluto anyway? Tim must have let him out when he came down get a glass of water—and left him out there. He must be freezing! Nigel and Pluto, here I come.

Uh-oh—the garage is open. Tim must have forgotten to close it after his bike ride last night. I hope his bike's not been stolen Lord, that would be awful! Just as well I did leave the lid on Nigel as there are foxes everywhere.

Few minutes later…

OH NO!

Went to the garage to get Nigel out—but he's been ripped to bits, and is strewn in a trail across our filthy garage floor! Not only that, he's covered in gravel and green grains of mouse poison and slug pellets. In other words, totally inedible, Lord!

At first I thought it was foxes—but when I saw Pluto in the corner with brine-soaked peppercorns and star anise in his beard, looking sick and guilty, I thought, oh no Pluto, it was you!

PLUTO HAS MAULED NIGEL, LORD!

He must have gone in the garage, been driven mad by the smell of Nigel in the Tupperware, nudged off the lid, dragged him out and scoffed him!

This is all Tim's fault, Lord! He left garage door open and forgot to bring Pluto back in!

How-o-how can I be an O.W. Lord, when things like this happen? I make heart-felt prayers with the best of intentions—then two seconds later something like this happens and it drives me around the bend!

What are we going to do? Everyone's arriving in a few hours' time and there's nothing to eat!

Don't know whether to laugh, cry, or go to get the fish fingers out of the freezer. (Definitely no chance of anyone getting salmonella now).

R.I.P. Nigel.

8pm

Panic over. Christmas Dinner fine in end. In a way, the turkey drama welded us all together. We had sausages, bacon, buckets of gravy and the Quorn burgers Liz gave us months ago with an air of triumph that only comes in the face of such adversity.

Imogen arrived with a nut roast too. She's split up with Mark again, this time 'for good'. She had to park down the lane as WGM did shoot into my nicely cleared space while we were at church.

9pm

A funny thing has just happened, Lord. I went upstairs in a 100% dedicated fashion to hang up a tie Tim's parents had bought for him, when I came across a piece of paper stuck to his wardrobe door, behind the other ties. A list of the promises he made when he married me. I've never noticed them before.

Always, always tell her she looks beautiful

Regularly buy her perfume, shoes and dresses and book at least 25 mystery long weekends away a year

Crack at least ten jokes a day and make it my mission to make her laugh and 100% happy for the rest of her life

If it's pouring and there are big puddles everywhere, take off my coat and put it on the pavement so she doesn't get her feet wet

Love her as I do my own body... sacrificing all for her

Consider her better than myself.

Lord! We've *both* made lists of promises! Some of the good, some of them... crazy! I guess we didn't need to make lists at all.

I must show them to Tim later, so we can have a good laugh.

Lord, I wonder if Tim has kept a diary too?

The END

Please see over

Thank you for reading

If you have enjoyed this book and have a minute, please review it on Amazon or Goodreads and please tell your friends about it.

Get in touch with Karola on Social Media

Follow her at Twitter.com/karolawoods
Like her page at Facebook.com/writingkarola

About the author

Karola became a Christian on holiday to New York in the late 90s. She went to a gospel service in Harlem with her sister and was bowled over by the worship. It was 100% alive and not boring at all. When she turned to her sister (who was already a Christian) to say, 'Have you seen anything like this before?' she saw her standing there with her hands outstretched and her eyes closed, focusing on God. At that moment, Karola realised this was what she wanted too. Her heart was changed in an instant and when she returned to the UK, she started attending a lively church and gave her life to Jesus. You too can do the same, you'll never regret it. It's not about religion, it's about a real relationship with God. Just say sorry for your sins and accept Jesus the Son of God into your heart as your Lord and Saviour, who died for you and rose again. Life following Him will never be boring and will never ever be the same again!

Karola has also written the comedy 'Are My Roots Showing?' also available on Amazon. It has lots and lots of 5* reviews.

Printed in Great Britain
by Amazon